# Footsteps Judea

MY JOURNEY IN KRAV MAGA
AND LIFE

## Volume 4

*Writings From 2015*

*By*

## Moshe Katz

*Israeli Krav International*
www.israelikravinternational.com

*Maaleh Adumim, Israel*

*Published by*

*IKI – Israel*

*At*

*CreateSpace*

ISBN: 13: 978-1541379961
Copyright © 2017 by Moshe Katz

Footsteps from Judea by Moshe Katz
www.israelikravinternational.com

# Table of Contents

Table of Contents ............................................................. 3

Introduction .................................................................. 8

First Impression ............................................................. 9

Hitting and Talking ........................................................ 13

I Was Asked a Question ................................................. 17

Suitcase Contents .......................................................... 23

Happy or Mad Krav Maga Training ................................. 26

The Dead Listen and Speak ............................................. 29

What Would I Do? .......................................................... 33

Little People .................................................................. 36

Promises We Cannot Keep .............................................. 39

Roots and Branches ....................................................... 61

Ranks, Titles, and Respect in Krav Maga ........................ 64

Think Ahead .................................................................. 67

Charred Remains ........................................................... 71

Martial Arts Ornamentation .......................................... 75

Old Teachers ................................................................. 79

Old Lessons ................................................................... 82

Sports Self Defense ....................................................... 85

Fences and Krav Maga ................................................... 88

Clear Language .............................................................. 91

Train No Exit ................................................................. 97

| | |
|---|---|
| A Soft Breeze Blows | 100 |
| Krav Maga Sparring | 103 |
| The Cobbler, Adam Sandler | 106 |
| Find A Path | 109 |
| Twenty-Five Years | 112 |
| Beginners Luck | 115 |
| Be True to Yourself, Keep Your Balance | 122 |
| And Moses Spoke | 124 |
| Truth or Not | 127 |
| Pride, Fall, and Modesty | 130 |
| Changes | 132 |
| Can't Buy Me Experience | 135 |
| The Nature of Evil | 138 |
| Stories from Life, Krav Maga Works | 141 |
| Hysteria or Clear Thinking | 147 |
| Krav Maga Gentle Warriors | 150 |
| Employee or Leader | 154 |
| Getting Good at It | 158 |
| Be the Storm | 160 |
| One Man's Perspective | 163 |
| Who Are You? | 165 |
| Grandfather-Godfather | 170 |
| Hands Up Baby | 173 |
| Got Skills | 176 |

| | |
|---|---|
| Class Act | 179 |
| Guarantees | 186 |
| Realistic Expectations | 189 |
| Clouds | 192 |
| Krav Leadership Challenges | 195 |
| Honor Among Thieves | 199 |
| Easy Money | 203 |
| Feeling Proud | 205 |
| Krav Maga Control and Goals | 207 |
| The Best Defense | 211 |
| Organizational Planning | 214 |
| My Friend Zack | 217 |
| Krav Maga and the Mona Lisa | 221 |
| Zuz | 228 |
| First Line of Defense | 229 |
| Different ways of training in Krav Maga | 232 |
| Social Media and Krav Maga | 234 |
| Ask Questions | 237 |
| Rapid Cure | 240 |
| Krav Maga Joy | 244 |
| Kadima - Forward | 247 |
| Understand the Student | 250 |
| Krav Maga Quality Control | 252 |
| The Price We Pay | 254 |

| | |
|---|---|
| Feeling Proud | 257 |
| See the Future | 260 |
| The Gentle Way | 265 |
| Krav Maga - Build On Weakness | 271 |
| Do Not Turn Back | 275 |
| Intelligence and Faith | 278 |
| Benefit of Doubt | 281 |
| Quick to Judge | 284 |
| Pride and Fall | 287 |
| When Children Play | 289 |
| Truth is Painful | 292 |
| Adapting Adjusting Defense | 297 |
| Age of Distraction | 301 |
| A Thousand Miles | 305 |
| Lowest Common Denominator | 307 |
| Philosopher's Table | 310 |
| Faith | 313 |
| Peace - Yehi Shalom | 318 |
| Connection | 321 |
| Quitters and Winners | 325 |
| Pharaoh's Peace | 328 |
| It Must Be Right | 332 |
| Better Judgment | 336 |
| Searching and Finding | 338 |

| | |
|---|---|
| I Was Sent Before You | 341 |
| Awareness Look | 345 |
| Songs and Guns | 348 |
| Historical Vision | 351 |
| Listen Well | 354 |
| Misunderstandings | 359 |
| Dare to Be Different | 362 |
| Memories and Lessons | 366 |

# Introduction

This book is a collection of my thoughts, my sparks, my journeys of this past year that I want to share with you. It is meant to inspire, to provoke, to sooth, to wake up, as a comfort and as a call to action. It is my attempt to deal with the human condition and the struggles that we all share. It is also my way of sharing the lessons I have gained over my lifetime. It has been my privilege to meet and learn from some great people. I share with you those experiences. And just as these role models shared their teachers' stories with me I share them with you; passing on the torch. Take a walk with me, into the past, into the future, into the known, and into the unknown.

*Moshe Katz, December 30, 2016*

# First Impression

JUNE 30, LOS ANGELES, CALIFORNIA, USA

I like California. People say that LA is superficial but I don't find that to be the case. Believe it or not I find the people here easy going, sincere and honest. And no, I am not a fool.

People are relaxed and not trying to make an impression. Of course this is not true of everyone. But overall, after having lived here and having visited yearly for many years I can say that I find that people are what they are, truly genuine, they are not trying to make an impression.

They dress as they want, talk as they want, relaxed, causal. They have their own style, their own way, I find it sincere.

Yes, California is laid back, there is that certain energy; I feel it every time I am here. Just be you, be real.

Walking into a store and being greeted like a long lost best friend at first seemed fake, but not anymore. Once I learned to trust people a little bit more I find that they are just good people. Yes, there is something unique here about the culture, the friendly person at the store might actually just be a good person, and that friendly help is sincere, not just a sales pitch.

The positive energy is contagious. The good feeling makes it a real pleasure to come back here.

Bruce Lee said something very similar. *"Freedom discovers the man the moment he losses concern over the impression he is making or about to make"*

*Showing off is the fool's idea of glory* (Bruce Lee)

I find that here in California people are less about trying to impress anyone. Like the Dude in **The Big Lebowski**, they are who they are, and that is all they are. People are pretty open, natural, easy.

And of course this fits in perfectly with the IKI Krav Maga way of thinking, which is totally at odds with other styles of Krav Maga. We start off from a completely different point and we end up at different points.

We are not at all about making an impression. We are not into the *Tough Guy Bad Ass image* that the others work so hard to cultivate.

When people meet me, they do not guess I am a Krav Maga instructor; I am not big, no tattoos or huge muscles, no "tough talk". I am a quiet mild mannered regular guy.

And so are most of you.

At IKI we are not about making an impression. We have matured past that, we are beyond that. We are free of that hang-up.

I personally have no need to impress anyone.

I impressed my teacher enough to be the only person ever to be awarded a 4th *dan* black belt by him. I have impressed the world martial arts community enough to be awarded a 6th *dan* black belt and numerous international awards. I have impressed myself enough not to have to make any impression on you.

All I care about now, is you, the student. For too many Krav Maga schools the goal is to impress: The teacher wants to totally impress his students so that they will worship him. The student wants to impress the teacher and win his blessing and approval. But what does any of this amount to?

When God forbid a deranged ex-boyfriend or girlfriend walks into your house with a gun and points it at you, point blank range, what does your dojo image matter??

**Side note**: When we train we get questions from beginners who lack real life experience, who simply do not understand reality. Why, they ask, would anyone get so close to you with the gun? It makes no sense!

I always answer that we are not dealing with professional killers but with an angry person, they want to intimidate, so they get up close. And that is what happened to the dear relatives of one of our new members, back in December. Tragic. So we train for this, we do not train to impress anyone.

I know our Krav Maga is real, pure, authentic and honest. It is based on instinct, natural reactions and gross motor moves. It is not designed to make any impression on anyone, it is designed for your survival and nothing else.

Impress your family by staying alive and coming home safe.

*Always be yourself, express yourself, have faith in yourself, do not go out and look for a successful personality and duplicate it.* (Bruce Lee)

# Hitting and Talking

### July 2, Los Angeles, Ca, USA

We read the story of Moshe, Moses, striking the stone and water coming forth to quench the thirst of the nation of Israel. It was a great miracle and yet, Moshe and his brother Aharon, were severely reprimanded and punished; they would not enter the Land of Israel, they would not enter the Promised Land.

They were punished because God said: "Speak to the rock", but Moshe hit the rock, instead. Perhaps, a slight miscommunication, these things happen; and yet such a terrible punishment.

After leading this stiff-necked people for forty years, putting up with the whining, the nagging, the complaining, Moshe and Aharon will not be privileged to enter themselves, they will not be the ones to lead the Nation of Israel into its homeland.

Ever since that day, generations of rabbis have pondered this question; why?

What was so terrible? Why were they punished this way?

This past Shabbat I heard some interesting commentary from Rabbi Adato here in Los Angeles. He mentioned that the situation is even more confusing in that earlier Moshe was commanded by God to, in fact, hit the rock and bring forth water, so why was it such a big deal that this time he hit the rock, instead of speaking to it, as God had commanded him.

The rabbi explained that earlier, the nation of Israel had been on a lower spiritual level, they had just left Egypt, they had not yet experienced the Divine revelation at Mount Sinai, they had not yet met God and received his words.

But, after all those experiences, God did not want Moshe to hit, he wanted Moshe to talk. The people were now on a higher spiritual level.

This idea, immediately resonated with me and I felt once again the Biblical Krav Maga connection.

Talking is the higher level. Imagine if all people could talk things out, wouldn't that be terrific!

Indeed that is the higher level, use your words not your fists or guns or nuclear weapons. But sadly, in many cases, that is not our reality. So, the rabbi is correct. After seeing God, one should be on a higher level, one should be free of violence, but we certainly cannot count on it.

So, for now, keep training.

But there is more.

A few days later, I bumped into the rabbi again and we talked about the Torah lessons and the connection to Krav Maga. He made another interesting point.

He said that the hitting came first, and only later there was talking. There is a powerful lesson here. In order for the talk to have any power, it must be preceded by and backed up by force, by hitting.

Diplomacy works much better when the enemy knows you have a powerful army to back up your words. Passivity has never won any wars. The lesson is clear, if you want peace - prepare for war.

If you want personal security - prepare for personal violence.

*Comments*

Moshe: Just a note on your post about hitting/talking. I can speak with absolute authority to the accuracy of your words. I have had at least three, probably four situations that could have turned very ugly and very physical, none of which I started. Fortunately, all of these occurred well after I started training seriously. I believe the confidence one develops from (serious) training develops an "aura" that aggressors notice. In each of these cases I was able to stay calm, keep my tone of voice very calm and moderated, think clearly and ask questions to try to diffuse the situation. I also positioned myself so that anything the aggressor might do could be easily dealt with but not close enough to "invite" physical contact. Interestingly, by not allowing the verbal aggression to escalate and by not becoming overtly confrontational or defensive or offensive, the aggressor in each case finally backed away and left. I never moved in any direction but rather just calmly stood my ground and relaxed. The flip side was that in each case I was studying his "body English" deciding whether he was likely right or left handed, etc., and figuring what I would do in the event he decided to attack in various ways.... As you cite in your book, when negotiating for peace one must also be preparing for war. I was never, even for a second, worried about the situation which seems a little strange but it is true.

One relative comment I have posed to you before: Confidence is great if it is real...cockiness will get you hurt or killed very quickly.

Prior to training seriously, I would likely have been drawn into escalating the verbal aggression and no telling what might have happened.

# I Was Asked a Question

July 2, El Al, flight 6, Los Angeles - Israel

A work of art, the Lady in Gold, was, eventually, returned to its legal owner, Maria Altmann, but over 100,000 similar works of art have never been returned and are still in the possession of thieves, people who continue to profit from the Nazi era.

Neo-Nazism is on the rise, who will take a stand?

I was asked a question...

It was a year ago, It was a most honest question, a question that took courage to ask. It was an innocent question.

But this question showed an abysmal lack of knowledge, a glaring hole in one's historical perspective, an insensitivity that cries out to the heavens; a generation that forgot.

I was asked a question, a question born of ignorance, ignorance that can hardly be forgiven.

I was asked a question, by a young German woman. She is certainly not an anti-Semite, she is not a hater, but she is part of a new generation that is often obtuse when it comes to the painful past. I have seen this all over Europe, in particular in France - *a country that greatly aided the Nazis in their extermination of the Jews of their country.* I have seen young people who do not understand the unique suffering of the Jews. These people prefer to live in a Fantasy Land, a fairy tale where "there were a few bad people", but all is good now and "let's stop living in the past".

But this is not true, they are wrong, on this point there can be no discussion.

I was asked a question...

Her question was not only her own, she asked me in the name of others, her friends back in Germany. They simply did not understand. Perhaps they could not understand, not until they come to Israel, not until they walk a mile in our shoes, a mile that runs through Masada, the sites of ancient battles and Yad Va Shem Holocaust Memorial.

I was asked a question...and it startled me that any European could be so clueless about their past.

I was asked a question and it shocked me that they could be so uninformed about our lives.

I was asked.... Why does the German government still have to pay this generation of Jews Holocaust reparations?

By the end of her stay, she fully understood the answer, after long discussions and her participation in Tour and Train Israel Experience, she came around completely. Now she acts as a spokesperson on behalf of the Jewish people of Israel, now she no longer asks, now she explains to others. She continues to visit Israel and to train here with the best.

But I suspect that her audience still does not understand. They must come here.

They *must* come here.

To come to terms with themselves, they must come here and live with us for a while. They must complete the journey.

### A little history

Everyone talks about the destruction of over six million Jews in Europe during World War Two, crimes committed by the Nazis and their very willing accomplices in many countries, but there is more.

What many ignore is that along with the lives lost, much property was lost. The property of millions of Jews, the bank accounts, the homes, business and art works, valued at many billions of dollars, was also stolen. Add to this the "back-pay" for slave labor.

On suffering and death there can be no price, but on property there can be.

In September 1951, Chancellor Konrad Adenauer of West Germany, addressed his Parliament: "... *unspeakable crimes have been committed in the name of the German people, calling for moral and material indemnity ... The Federal Government are prepared, jointly with representatives of Jewry and the State of Israel ... to bring about a solution of the material indemnity problem, thus easing the way to the spiritual settlement of infinite suffering.*"

This lead to what became known in Israel simply as "reparations". I used to work in a bank in Jerusalem. I recall at a certain time each month, elderly Jews with foreign accents would come in, to collect their reparations, a small monthly stipend from the German government.

Contrary to the understanding of our young German friend it is not "The Jews" who receive this stipend, but only Survivors who can prove what they have lost. The vast overwhelming majority of the financial losses of the Jewish people of Europe, have never been recovered. What we have received is not even a drop in the ocean, an ocean of Jewish tears.

The minimal sums that are still received, are used by elderly survivors to cope on a daily basis. Many of them live below the poverty line. Many have to choose between using the heat in winter or buying the medications they need. They must choose between buying a new shirt, or having lunch.

I said to my young German friend, in as calm a way as I could: "Imagine, your father owned a textile factory, was a self-made wealthy man. He owned the entire apartment building and collected rent. He owned an art collection. Your mother and grandmother owned gold jewellery. But then the Nazis came and stole everything, your family was deported and killed but you alone survived. And now you live alone in a small apartment in Israel. You live with your memories, your trauma, your fears and anxiety.

You live on a small government stipend, which is barely enough to cover your basic needs. All you are asking from the German people is a little extra, to pay for heat on a cold day, to cover the cost of your medications, to have enough to eat. And...

I was asked a question.... Why do we still need to pay "The Jews"

Why? Because they are still suffering, because there are no "survivors", no one has really "survived". There are Witnesses to the greatest crime ever, there are people who emerged physically not dead, but there is no one who truly survived.

To this day, every survivor suffers; they, their children, their grandchildren and all of us. As one Israeli said: "the Holocaust is in our DNA", we still live it.

I have a relative, let's call her Rachel. She was only a child when "It" happened. Her parents were taken away, fate unknown to this very day. She survived four concentration camps. Today she is old, she lives in fear. Every night the ghosts come to life, the Nazis are still there, in her nightmares. She cannot be alone. She calls for her children who must travel long distances to be with her. Who is paying for those flights? Who is paying for her children to miss work?

She can no longer be alone. She cannot walk alone, she lives in fear. And she is called a "survivor".

An old woman sits in an apartment in Tel Aviv, she is cold, she suffers from injuries sustained at Auschwitz, she dreams of her family as they were before the war, she dreams of their home in Germany, of the lifestyle they led, she remembers her father in a fine suit, playing the cello. Her bones ache, she feels chills, when she falls asleep she sees them: her family, humiliated, she sees Nazis in uniform barking at them, deciding who shall live and who shall die. And a young German asks; why are we still paying "the Jews".

# Suitcase Contents
### July 3-5, El Al, Israel

Wisdom can be found anywhere, if you keep your eyes and mind open.

Over the years, with hundreds of flights all over the world, I have had the frustrating experience of my suitcases being damaged and destroyed. Nothing like picking up your new suitcase at baggage claim and finding it torn, missing a wheel, handle ripped or zipper broken. At times, I have had to buy a new suitcase right there at the airport.

Finding just the right suitcase has been a real challenge. Buying new suitcases has become one of the many "hidden" expenses of travel, one of the "cost of doing business" expenses.

Checking into El Al at the Los Angeles airport, I see a disclaimer in English and Hebrew, it was cute, funny, accurate and wise.

It said something along the lines of ...*Remember that the purpose of your suitcase is to protect its contents. So if your suitcases come out with some nicks, dents, discoloration etc... keep that in mind.*

I had to laugh; in a way that was so Israeli, so much a part of who we are as a people. As the rabbis said so long ago - do not look at the jar, look at the contents.

That is life in Israel. I was chatting with Esther, I told her that in the El Al business lounge all the Israeli businessmen were dressed in sweatpants and baggy T-shirts, whereas the Japanese, are in business suits and ties.

*"Doesn't it make more sense to travel comfortably? The Israeli way?"*

Yes, it does, content over appearance. With El Al you can never tell who is rich or poor, who is a businessman and who is a backpacker.

Look at the inside of the person, not the exterior. We have always valued content over appearance. As my grandfather had written on every book he owned: *"If you possess wisdom, what do you lack? If you lack wisdom, what do you possess?"*

How true. Thank you El Al for the reminder. And I am OK with that, even though I only bought my newest suitcase two trips ago and now it already looks worn out and used: The cost of doing business. The purpose of the suitcase is to protect the contents and contents were all safe.

*Content over appearance*

And that is the essence of IKI Krav Maga.

People have criticized us that on video, our style does not "look so tough". Sometimes the simplicity of our style makes it look "easy". We have no need to appear tough or beat people up. In addition, unlike other styles of Krav Maga, we do not create the artificial distinction between so called civilian Krav Maga and military Krav Maga.

We do not care what kind of impression we are making, that is the suitcase, the exterior, the protection. We care only about the content, you: that is your ability to survive a violent personal attack and get home safe.

Remember, no flash and trash. No fake acting and choreography (leave that to Hollywood, Please!!)

Content is all that matters, with suitcases and with your life.

# Happy or Mad Krav Maga Training

JULY 5, 2015 ISRAEL

There are different definitions of reality training; there are different definitions of what it means to be strong. Some of the strongest people I have known over the years could not win an arm-wrestling match and some of the physically strongest were those who needed to be carried by others.

Julie San - "I am not very strong"

Mr. Miyagi - "Many kinds of strong Julie San" (Karate Kid part 4)

There are different ideas of how it is best to train. I remember one traditional Karate dojo where I used to train. They treated it like a secret military facility. When one of the instructors discovered that I was taking pictures, he came over and demanded my camera.

In another gym, the Thai boxing gym of Kru Phil Nurse, the situation was different. Phil is a champion in many weight classes and divisions, he is as tough as nails, could break your leg with one kick, but his greatest weapon is his smile. With one smile he can totally disarm you.

When he saw my camera, he too took it from me. Moments later I noticed him climbing the ring to take photos. He, the champion, was taking photos for me. I will never forget that.

Smiling does not make you less tough. Those who need to put up a facade are to be pitied.

When Yuriko and Ramon first came to my seminar in Argentina with Jose Nacul, they had already been training for many years. They said that after ten minutes they understood that their fourteen-hour bus ride was well worth it. How devoted.

One of the many differences they noted with our style is that we smile. We enjoy our training. Yuriko said that in her former style of Krav Maga, smiling was never allowed, it was seen as a sign of weakness. Krav Maga had to be hard, no smiling!

Of course, we know that a tea spoon of sugar helps the medicine go down, i.e. everything is easier if you are enjoying it.

But is there room for anger?

I believe there is. We need a balance between the two. We must find the correct balance.

I would never want to be a part of a class where the teacher was always angry or mad, or sad. Never. I think this would be a horrible environment to try and learn something. It would never work.

Most of the time we need to smile, to enjoy the training, to look forward to the training. Now and then we need to get a little "dark" and put some anger and fear into the training, to prepare us for the reality of an attack.

But I do believe that if the training environment is always filled with fear and anger, very little actual learning will take place.

Fear and intimidation has never proven to be a successful educational method.

*First seminar in Argentina, all happy faces and great training. With Jose Nacul, Yuriko and Ramon from Chile and IKI Argentina.*

# The Dead Listen and Speak

### July 6, 2015, Israel

One of those questions. Do the dead hear us? Do they know if we pray for them, speak to them?

Do they hear us, do they answer?

The living shall never know with certainty, but the conversation still goes on.

Radomsko, a little town in Poland, near Łódź, the hotel Zameczek knows how to keep a kosher kitchen to accommodate the Hasidim, the devout followers of the Radomsker Rebbe known as the *Tiferes Shlomo,* the first leader of this group, now long since dead.

The town of Radomsko was occupied and most of its Jews deported and killed during the German occupation of Poland during World War II. The fourth Radomsker Rebbe, Rabbi Shlomo Chanoch HaKohen Rabinowicz, was murdered by the Nazis in the Warsaw Ghetto in 1942, bringing the father-to-son dynasty to an end.

But the followers still come. They return to the place their *rebbes*, their spiritual leaders, lived and studied and prayed. And the local Polish population can't make any sense of it.

And we come. We come to Warsaw and we come to Ukraine, to Russia and Hungary and Slovakia, and we come to wherever our ancestors died, and we chat with them. It is more than paying our respect; it is an on-going conversation. We are telling them that as long as we keep their ways, their lives were not wasted; their deaths not in vain.

My great grandparents in Brooklyn, NY, bought a bench to be placed near their final resting place. They asked that the family visit, have a picnic and chat, like old times.

A visionary once told me that "the conversation still goes on". With us Jews, the conversation is never over.

But the dead do speak to us, in many ways. When my dear brother, Ethan, was going through the most difficult part of his IDF training, he felt the dead. He wrote to us that as he was crawling on his belly through a field filled with thorns, or a field of mud, he felt our people with him. What would a Jew in Poland have given to be in my shoes? He asked, to be wearing the uniform of the Israeli army, to be a proud soldier of Israel carrying the latest model rifle?

What would our ancestors have given to be in our boots?

Yes, they talk to us, and the question is, do we listen?

When I see a Jew who is detached from his people, his religion, his heritage and his glorious history, I understand; there can be only one reason, he has left the conversation, he has stopped listening.

For our ancestors are always with us, and they are always sending us messages. And the message is - do not forget us, do not forget what we struggled for, do not forget what we died for; do not forget who you are!

Do not be as Esau who sacrificed his birth right for a bowl of lentils.

The dead speak if we listen.

When my mother was a young girl she asked my grandfather, Rabbi Isaac Klein, of blessed memory: "Why does God no longer speak to us, like he did with our Biblical prophets?"

He answered wisely:

*"Hannah, do you own a radio?"*

*"Yes, Abba, (father), I do"*

*"Do you hear music now?"*

*"No, the radio is not turned on."*

*"Exactly, when the radio is turned off you cannot hear music, and when your heart is turned off, you cannot hear God speaking to you."*


The conversation never ends. We love to talk. But we also must learn to listen.

With Krav Maga we are also listening. We are listening to those who were not prepared, who had not followed the Biblical advice of "Pray for peace but prepare for war". We listen to those who died and implore us; do not be caught unprepared! Train to fight back.

We listen, we remember, and we prepare for a better future. Pray for peace, but prepare for war.

Still true after all these years.

# What Would I Do?

### July 7, 2015, Israel

What would you do if you had unlimited money? No financial worries, no need to earn a living? No bills to pay?

This is not merely a fantasy question, the answer, even if only hypothetical, tells a great deal about who we are; our core, our values.

Who are you??

For even if we never earn that million, if our ship never comes in, the dream remains, our goals, our values, are always with us.

To have a dream is to live. We Jews have lived with our dreams, and our faith.

*If I were a rich man* - sings Tevye, the classic Jew from *Fiddler on the Roof*...I would treat my family well, give money to the poor and most of all, most of all...spend seven hours every day with the learned rabbis, studying the holy books, sit in the synagogue and pray.
*Oy....Ahh...If I were a rich man.*

This tells us that though Tevye is a poor milkman, a poor Jew living in an exiled condition, never knowing when his Ukrainian, Russian, Latvian, Lithuanian... neighbors will turn on him, his dream is to devote time to sitting with the rabbis, the wise men and studying the holy books. Ahh. If I were a rich man....

There was a commercial for the Israeli lottery: each episode featured a different Israeli, answering the question: "what would you do if you won the lottery?"

An old Yemenite Jew, with traditional side-curls and prayer shawl says..."*I would build a large synagogue, three floors! One for Jews from Europe, one for Jews from Africa and one for Yemenite Jews*" (As each has its own tradition).

Ahh...such is the dream of an honest pious man, not personal gain, not personal glory, just the needs of the community. *If I were a rich man....* tells a lot about our character.

And what would I do? What would I, Moshe Katz, do?

*If I were a rich man.... If I were a wealthy man, I wouldn't have to work hard.*

But I would do the same thing, only differently.

IKI Krav Maga would continue, of course, but I would have more help. I would have full time help, I would make IKI better. I would make less mistakes with e mails, I would have a larger inventory of T shirts, the packages would go out faster, I would not accidentally book the same flight twice (Yes...has happened).

But I would, also, have more time for personal growth, as Tevye said.... *sitting with the rabbis seven hours every day, posing problems that would cross a rabbi's eyes.* Give to the community; continue the rich legacy of our people. Make the world a little bit safer for all...Heal the world, give people a sense of personal safety.

Yes, if I were a rich man, I would do exactly as I am doing now, only better.

Live a life worth a living, live your dream...

*Oy...If I were a rich man....*

I believe in what I do, I believe in what I teach. And I love it when IKI instructors offer something for free "to contribute to the cause". For yes, this is a cause. It is a cause so noble, that I would do it even, even if ...even if I were rich man!

# Little People
### July 13, 2015, Israel

History is about the big people. Read any history book and you will find the big names, the names of people whose actions shaped history.

Stalin, Churchill, Roosevelt, Hitler, Ivan the Great, Ivan the Terrible, Peter the Great, Catherine the Great, Napoleon, Harold the Great, Abraham Lincoln, Moses, Abraham, David.

We all know the big names. These people define history. But what about the other people, what about the little people?

History may record the "great" acts of the "great" leaders, but we forget the people who did the real work.

Great pyramids were built...on the back of poor slaves. Great cities were built, on the backs and bones of ordinary people. The wealth of the "great" leaders was sustained by the back breaking labor of the peasants. For one thousand years, the poor common Russian man and woman, paid for this wealth with their lives. Saint Petersburg was called the "City of Bones", as so many Russians died building it. Great cathedrals are still admired to this day, but do we stop and think of the human toll it took to build these buildings? No "politically correct" person today should ever step foot in those churches and cathedrals, the human toll and suffering it took to create these are staggering.

The truly great man or woman may not be the one you think of. We live in an era of opportunity and it is difficult for us to imagine a time when a man or a woman was bound to a piece of land for life and had no opportunities for change. Yet, these people, toiled and did their best to provide a decent life for their family.

Great generals are remembered, but the "cannon fodder", the millions of unknown soldiers are the ones who paid the price.

Power corrupts and the great leaders forget the little people.

There are exceptions, few exceptions, Alexander the Second, some of the American leaders, the French Revolution. But for the most part those in power, forget those who are not in power. The little people are forgotten and are left to fend for themselves.

The same is true today with big corporations. They care about profits, the stock holders, the big investors. But what about some poor little kid who is consuming something harmful? Who really cares?

The same is true of most sport and martial arts organizations. I have met with the leaders, the business managers, it is all about profit; how to make more money, how to take over a bigger share of the pie. Rarely is it about how to help more people.

Most martial arts clubs focus on the big names, someone who can win a tournament and bring "honor" to the school, (or more business), but what about a person who cannot afford lessons? What about the little people, in size, in financial ability, in physical ability; what about them?

Anyone who has trained with us knows that we care, that financial ability is never a factor, that physical ability is never a factor, that size, age, or gender, is never a factor. Those who know us: know.

We may not be able to change history, but yet, perhaps, we can. Perhaps each one of us who takes a little initiative, who makes a little effort, can change something.

We can begin by thinking of the little people, because all people matter.

# Promises We Cannot Keep

July 14, 2015, Israel

Keeping a promise is a virtue, a time honored value. In all societies, during all ages, this has not changed. A promise is a promise. Your word is your honor.

Sadly these days, I have heard of retreats and "seminars" where new age thinkers teach that promises are only to be kept as long as they serve your needs. When the promise no longer benefits the one who made it: it is off, you are absolved: Modern hogwash. (I was the victim of such a broken promise).

My dad, of blessed memory, would often comment on such situations. You made a mistake and sometimes, in order to keep your promise, your word, it is going to cost you. *"Ribe gelt"* he would say in Yiddish, roughly this means: learning money, the money you lost to learn a valuable lesson.

We want to make promises; we want to protect our loved ones. We want to reassure our young that we shall always be there for them, that we shall always protect them. But we must be careful, for once a promise is made, it must be kept.

Shortly after my father passed away, I was in Los Angeles visiting my brother and my nieces. The girls were watching the Lion King. I joined them for a few minutes. The young cub was in trouble with his dad, the Lion King, he had messed up. Soon all was straightened out and the relieved young lion said to his dad: "So Dad, we are OK?" and the father answered: "Yes, we are OK."

The exchange that followed next hit me hard. The cub continues: "And you will always be with me Dad?"

And my heart pounded. What could a father answer? The truth is a father cannot respond with a 'yes'. The father will die before the son. My father, my role model, my hero, had just died. If he could die, any father could die. So how could a father say: Yes, I will always be there for you?

But this is only a children's film, and yet, we cannot lie to children. What would the Lion King say?

My heart beat fast, all this happened in a split second. And then, the brilliant line: *"No son, I will not always be here for you, but I will always watch over you."*

Truer words have never been spoken.

The truth is we cannot always be there for the next generation, but we can do our utmost to protect them.

I recall a horrible scene. A young Israeli girl had been killed by an Arab terrorist. She was so young, so sweet, so innocent. She had not trained in Krav Maga, she was enjoying life and partying, not practicing to defend against knife attacks. What kind of world do we live in, where a teenage girl must worry about knife attacks? But we do.

I watched on the news, her poor mother was sobbing over her daughters' fresh grave: *"Forgive me daughter, I have failed you, forgive me for not protecting you."*

A parent cannot always be there to shield their child. And no teenager wants their parent to serve as a constant bodyguard. But what we can do, what we must do, is train them.

Just as a child must learn to read and write, they must learn to survive in the real world. Today that means Krav Maga. It is our obligation to train the next generation. Better to train them now then to apologize later. This is a promise we must make to the next generation, a promise we must keep. We cannot promise to always be there, but we must promise to prepare them to face life without us.

## July 2015

As the head instructor of IKI Krav Maga, I have made a promise to address every issue and every question raised by students/instructors/members of our organization.

The issue was recently brought to my attention of Krav Maga instructors, using live blades for training.

There are instructors out there, teaching various forms of self-defense or even calling it Krav Maga who are advocating a "sacrifice move" of grabbing a knife and allowing oneself to be cut "only on the dry skin of the palms".

In most countries there are no national boards certifying or overseeing Krav Maga instructors. Thus, anyone can rent a space and call themselves an instructor. New styles emerge every day.

Buyer beware.

Thus, it worries me when someone advocates using live weapons for self-defense training. There are people out there who might be turned on by this. There are people who might be drawn or attracted to this really "cool" stuff.

I am concerned about the idea of using real blades for training. My teacher was as tough as they come, but even he, never even suggested such an idea. Plastic/rubber knifes served us just fine.

I have written many blogs about the dangers of the blade.

Now I am not an EMT, but I have worked with many, I have been cut in several fights...but that was in a fight, in training, and I was prepared for it. I have also been accidentally cut by knives. I have had my share of work accidents. My question is ...What is the effect of being cut by a knife in a real-life altercation?

From what I have heard from students over the years, the effect is often, usually, total shock. We had a case with a short Italian fellow, attacked outside the Old City of Jerusalem by 3 larger Arabs. When he banged one of the attackers into the wall causing him to bleed, the two others ran off in a panic.

We had two students, elite security guards in Jerusalem, walking home after a shift, attacked by 5 Arabs, one of the Israeli guards used the magazine of his handgun as a knife, cut one of the Arabs on the cheek; all 5 Arabs fled at once.

So my thoughts are that when a regular person gets cut, unexpectedly, even such a non-lethal cut as these two cases above, people tend to panic. Under those circumstances it is difficult to imagine an effective martial arts defense.

The instructor in question, I have no idea who certified him if anyone, certainly no one in Israel advocates such training and this is not approved of either by Wingate or the IDF, suggests that one should grab the knife with his hands, not use the fingers, but use the palms and expect to get cut.

There is a similar video with this guy actually cutting himself to show that it is no big deal to bleed a little. (Please do not try this in class, certainly not an IKI approved idea at all).

Now let's think out loud. You have a knife to your throat, you grabbed it. How can you grab without using your fingers? For a baseball player to hit a baseball, he must grab the bat firmly with all 10 fingers. If one finger is broken, I can guarantee you that he will not be allowed to play until he is fully healed. Why? Because you need all ten fingers to form a solid reliable grip.

Back to our knife situation: You grabbed without letting the fingers come near the knife...unlikely to work to say the least. But let's assume for a moment that it does. Now a sharp blade is cutting your palms. My guess is that you will feel it, see it and this will cause you to weaken your grip, to slip. At this point, your fingers are next and they cut easily. So now, with bloody hands, cut fingers, you are trying to subdue an angry aggressive assailant. (try opening a bottle when you have greasy or oily hands).

Am I the only one who thinks this is insane?

I have seen people get cut and hurt with rubber training knives. I have discontinued using those knives and upgraded to safer knives.

We had a member in South Africa who advocated using real knives. He is now no longer part of our organization. We do not want you to get hurt on the street or in the dojo!

I have seen many bad techniques out there, many things I totally disagree with. But this has crossed all sane boundaries.


**YOUR COMMENTS AND INPUT ARE BELOW:**

Moshe

Experts have written that when it comes to knife wounds or gunshot wounds there are simply way no many variables and different situations to be able to properly answer the question: What will happen.

"The problem with answering these questions is that almost anything can happen. A gunshot wound can be a minor flesh wound, or it can be immediately fatal — usually if it enters the heart, the brain, on the upper portion of the spinal cord. The gunshot wound could cause damage to internal organs such as the lungs or liver and the victim could bleed to death rapidly, or slowly, or not at all. The same can be said of knife wounds and blunt trauma. Ask any emergency room physician and they will tell you that these types of injuries come in 1000 flavors."

*Dr. Kathrine Ramsland*

### OUR INSTRUCTORS SPEAK

Moshe,

Being a paramedic and bodyguard I have seen multiple stab wounds and the people who have a better rate of survival, when and only when they are able to stay calm. This is so VERY difficult for the average person given the significant trauma that the blade creates physically and mentally. Also, depending on where the victim is cut is dependent upon what we refer to as the GOLDEN HOUR of trauma and in that hour how much blood is lost. This will give you some idea on how long you have before you are physically incapacitated to the point of blackout or ultimately death.

Hope this helps.

Most Respectfully,

*Channel, Florida, USA*

Huge mistake; there are techniques where you grab the blade, I have done it, I have been through that training but I only teach it as a last resort and never with a live blade, most knives, even sharp will not cut you in less you get that back to back saw motion going, I have pried live blades out of people's hands with blade against the palm, typically it will not even cut your fingers if your fingers are touching , but that is a master level of training and we do that behind closed doors with a select group, he is asking for a serious lawsuit if he is telling people that is OK, nowadays to get cut with a live blade can also be death even on the hands, countries where all criminals use blades like South Africa, the blades can be infected with all sorts of disease including HIV / AIDS , criminals are not going to sterilize the blade after an attack or fight, Stoffel told me to get cut by a knife in SA can be a death sentence even if you survive the attack

*John Liptak, Florida, USA*


Hi Moshe

Interesting that someone cuts himself to prove.... what? he bleeds?. How about a demonstration to show us all how easy it is to cut a tendon and render a limb useless or maybe sever a nerve to permanently disable a hand. A little nick to prove one bleeds is just a macho attempt at proving toughness, it actually proves that the instruction is based on delusion and I will explain why,

1. Go to any kitchen draw and you will find knives that are razor sharp, when I say razor sharp I mean the blade is used for slicing.

2. A blade that is grabbed is a blade that can be pulled away by its holder and a pressure hold on a blade will not stop it slicing through flesh and bone.

3.When a tendon is cut the finger or fingers cease to work, I know this because I have a thumb that has tendon issues and it does not work.

Today we have people who will go to any lengths to kill or maim, these people don't carry blunt knives that can be grabbed ..... they carry razor sharp weapons that will slice and dice flesh, this is reality.

Best regards

*Tony Preston, England*


Considero desde mi humilde opinión. Que en un hecho real, coger la hoja del cuchillo, es un recurso desesperado, por haber fallado la persona en su entrenamiento y preparación adecuada en krav magá.

Y en ocasiones por imitar ejemplos de videos o películas.

*Filemón Almaraz Morales, Mexico*


Hello Moshe,

I read with interest your comments. As you know I am a serving police officer and before this I did 5 years working as a bouncer in the pubs and nightclubs of Essex and East London.

In these capacities, I have seen many people who have been attacked with a whole plethora of objects, from a pint glass, bottles, claw hammers, baseball bats and knives to name a few. I have seen some attacks unfold in front of my eyes and some I have turned up at the bloody aftermath.

No attack was the exactly the same and neither was the way the victims reacted, and here in lays the point of topic. It is my belief that certain factors come into play during such instances.

Firstly, how the adrenal syndrome will affect you. Whether you are induced into the fight or flight response, or whether you are one of the poor souls who freeze. Adrenalin is the body's natural defense mechanism and as well as making us stronger and faster in a fight it also gives us anaesthesia to pain.

Secondly your personal resolve. With a cast iron spirit you may override the fear aspect and it will also let you carry on when injured. (Although this is easier with people who are regularly exposed to being in this fear state. Police, security, military, trained fighters etc.) however I have seen ordinary blokes keep fighting with some very bloody injuries.

Thirdly drugs and alcohol. If you have a guy who has had 3 lines of coke and 5 pints of lager on a Friday night then he does not fight and react to pain in the same way as someone who is not high.

I remember speaking to one chap once who had been stabbed twice in the back and who was covered in blood however he did not know he was stabbed during the fight. He initially though he had just been punched hard in the back. Obviously, the wound was not to a vital area.

The real things which stop people are incapacitation (death, unconsciousness or use of noxious liquid or gas such as CS gas or pepper spray although this is not 100% on everyone) and severe limb damage (break or dislocation) to a major limb. (Not small digit manipulation like fingers and toes).

If this happens then the fight or attack normally stops.

Here I believe is the crux of the debate. In my experience I don't think we can say that if a blade is grabbed then 100% of people will react in X, Y, Z, of a way mentally.

However....... What is a given is that the likelihood of grabbing a sharp blade using the hands will in all probability result in damage to the muscle and tendons which control flexion of the hand, damage to the nerves of the hand or in a worst case damage the ulnar or radial arteries which supply the framework of blood vessels in the hand. (However, I have been told this would be difficult as they are deep seated in the hand).

Fights are dynamic, there is movement and this could cause cuts when gripping. This is not a training scenario in a dojo!

So, Yes, you might get the knife off the attacker doing this defense or it might go horribly wrong and because of the injury caused from grabbing the knife you freak out or damage the hand preventing use of the hand and in the end, lose the knife anyway. Either way you're either dead or have an injury to your hand from the grab that it's life changing physically.

Why take the risk. So why then court this type of defense when there are better techniques out there?

If you see people have a go at knife defense with no insight into any techniques. They result in either clinching the attacker and getting stabbed multiple times or they grab the arm, wrist or knife and end up missing or losing control. Again, ending up being stabbed.

We are the educated and use brains as well as Brawn. Why take the risk?

This obviously is my personal opinion using some real-life experience and I'd like to know what others think as well.

Keep safe buddy, speak soon.

*Brad. England.*


I'm with Moshe on this one. While I guess some people, who don't see and work with blood every day may get "squeamish" and run away or lose heart, I certainly wouldn't depend on that, and I suspect that someone who is attacking you with a weapon would be even less likely than an untrained citizen to exhibit that response.

Grip is the next consideration. Blood is slippery, drying blood is tacky; I know because I work with and in it every day. Having blood on your hands, especially the gripping palmar surface, will most likely cause your grip on a weapon to be less secure. I can't see any benefit in that.

As far as the hands and how they function, the palm is infinitely more complex and complicated than the dorsum (back) of the hand. Through the palm run the flexor tendons, which must be intact to allow for gripping and fist-making. Branches of the median, radial, and ulnar nerves also course beneath the palmar skin, and provide important sensation and dexterity to the fingers. If these nerves and tendons are injured, the hand becomes useless for anything other than a slapping tool. Conversely, the extensor tendons run along the dorsum (back) of the hand, and are superficially located. If severed, you will lose the ability to fully extend the fingers (as in a military salute), but flexion and grip will still be possible to allow you to fight more effectively. While no injury is welcome, an extensor tendon injury is vastly preferred over a flexor one for the immediate ability to continue functional fighting, and are relatively easy to repair later, in contrast to a flexor injury, which is much more technically difficult to repair and prone to complications. For these reasons, I was always taught by my Kali instructor to protect the palm at all costs, using the dorsum of the hand to deflect the attacker's forearm during our knife defense work.

As far as continuing to fight when injured, I believe we're all familiar with the body alarm response and the release of adrenaline, endorphins, and enkephalins, which allow us all to continue, sometimes unaware, despite sustaining an injury. Assailants high on stimulants and hallucinogens are another consideration and may render pain-compliance techniques useless. However, severed flexor tendons will still render a hand useless, no matter how jacked up the victim is. Stimulant or analgesic intoxication cannot overcome destruction of function; for this reason, the pelvis is taught in many circles as a primary target for pistol and rifle shot placement on an advancing attacker. It is not an immediate kill shot like a brainstem shot, but the assailant will stop. No degree of drug intoxication will enable an attacker to walk or run with a shattered pelvic girdle.

Based on the above reasoning, the concept of purposefully cutting or allowing oneself to be cut, especially on the palm, seems ridiculous to me. I hope this helps, and am looking forward to meeting Moshe at GMKM's upcoming seminar.

*AB, ER doctor, student of Hal Herndon, Ga, USA*

Moshe,

Training with loaded guns or real knives is not only dangerous but stupid. One mistake could result in the death or serious injury to a student or instructor. Not to mention it is a lawsuit waiting to happen, where the gym owner and instructor could be charged with a crime, assault with a deadly weapon or man slaughter. There is no kind of liability waiver that would protect those involved.

Sincerely,

*Taves Maciel, Colorado, USA*


Moshe,

Here are my thoughts...this behavior is unacceptable. In all seriousness, why intentional sacrifice any part of your body when you may need any part of your body as a means of self-defense?

Also, the probability of getting cut is already high in defending against a knife why increase the odds. You would have to be very accurate to only get cut on the "dry side" of the palm. If you miss and accidentally move the knife near the pointing finger and thumb you just cut through a main artery. Not a chance I want to take!

Statistical facts prove that a cut as shallow as 3mm can cause shock. In some fighting systems using weapons it is recommended to slash the extremities and or forehead. Not because it is deadly but because of the "shock" factor.

*Gary Bril. Florida*

Moshe,

Wow. Again, very disturbing to hear this is happening. As a nurse and Krav Maga instructor, I can see many things wrong with teaching this. I do tell my students that during any kind of knife defense, there is a chance you may get cut. However, it is something that we must try to do everything we can to avoid. It should be a priority to protect your vital organs as well as arteries in defending yourself. While your hands do not contain any major arteries, they are still necessary tools you need to defend yourself. You brought up many good points as to why we should not intentionally grab a blade with our hands. I completely agree.

*Carrie Banton, USA*


hi Moshe

wooowwww, this is crazy, unacceptable.

To grab the blade ... and get injured ... so if you are not trained in this scenario ... I think you will lose this fight also your live.

Maybe special forces – which train to get hurt, they can deal with this situation... but? is it necessary? NO!

A cut in the palm means ... mostly a cut in important anatomical structures ... a cut in the palm – and you cannot make a fist ... your fingers will open and the hand is weak.

Many people are collapsing when they see that they are bleeding ... so how to fight back if you are collapsed.????

You know I am a professional Nurse and I am trained as a bodyguard ... so I can deal with blood and also with pain ... but is this a reason to accept to get injured??? NEVER! If he cuts my right hand – the strong one – so what is my defense??

I am not able to punch, not able to hold a gun and not able to fight with a knife ...

I think everyone of us can grab a knife with full power ... and nothing will happen – no cut! ... but if the opponent moves the knife maybe about one inch ... you get a cut!

What about Nurses and Doctores in Hospital ... there are many surgery knifes ... they are not comparable with a Knife ... they are much much sharper ... if you grab the blade ... you get a cut- a deep cut...

shavoua tov

*Juergen, Germany*


Greetings Moshe,

I hope and pray that you are doing well my brother.

I wanted to offer a perspective on your latest "Blood" blog...

It is quite silly to me that someone would really think you need to train with a real knife to get a "real" training experience. There is no reason that an individual couldn't put some gear on and work with another responsible level headed partner and train in realistic knife defense. Martial arts have always attracted insecure individuals who are trying to compensate for some insecurity through talking tough or performing senseless acts of high risk training. Insecurity can become a person's greatest liability as they overcompensate to try to prove to themselves and others that they are really "the man". Their pride will become a liability to themselves, to those they may be protecting and to any who learn from them. Ultimately, I think that is what is at issue here more than the technique. The appropriately motivated protector would not concede to take such a risk in training that could permanently handicap themselves or others. I believe more important than anyone's skill, athleticism, speed etc., is their motivation and maturity. The best skills and techniques are useless when dominated by a mindset that is reckless and immature.

I am all for making training as realistic as possible as long as it stays safe to all who are participating. I think it is of utmost importance that we train in realistic means so we are not fooled into thinking our techniques are fool proof when they have only been used against cooperative partners. However, this does not mean loaded guns, live blades, and an out for blood mentality. I would severely question the character of individuals training in that manner.

I am with IKI because you Moshe have the right motivation. Your techniques are great and you embody the heart of a true protector. I believe the mark of a good instructor first and foremost is good character and maturity. The "tough guys" that are instructors only to be in front of people for their own validation should not have a place in your organization or any for that matter. We can't control them, but we can uphold what we stand for. Thank you for your faith based perspective that seeks to honor God by protecting life and upholding righteous principles.

Faithfully,

*Colby Taylor, Michigan, USA*


Moshe,

I am a trained and licensed EMT and have limited knowledge about this, for what it's worth. I have three things to suggest here:

1. The sight of blood does tend to shock and scare people (especially those who are not used to seeing it), as you stated. So being cut and seeing blood can cause a person to lose focus on his or her attacker. With the elevated heart rate and blood flow that necessarily accompanies a physical confrontation, bleeding would tend to be increased, causing even greater shock.

2. Building on the idea of the increased heart rate and blood flow during a physical confrontation, it doesn't take long for a person to lose enough blood for a cut to be fatal if not treated immediately. So, I don't believe that willingly accepting a cut to ANY part of the body is wise.

And there is no way to guarantee that a cut will be confined to the "dry skin" of the palms, as you stated in your original post.

3. My biggest concern here, added to your comments, is that a cut to the tendons of the palms or fingers renders the hands useless. A person should never sacrifice the hands in a fight (which is why I so appreciate your teachings about using the forearms and palms rather than fists in a fight).

I hope that helps in some way.

*Mike Jensen, Colorado, USA*


Moshe,

Let me just state that being from the medical community I would not advocate grabbing a knife with my hands, this will not end well and could risk permanent damage. Brings to mind a quote that I just posted the other day. "Everyone is born ignorant but one must work hard at remaining stupid."

*Greg D., Illinois, USA*


Hi Moshe, hope you are well.

I am actually writing this in response to your Blood Krav Maga blog. My story is from a little different perspective.

I cut someone in a fight 45 years ago, and I remember it as clearly as if it were this morning. It was a stupid, stupid mistake, I don't even remember what started it. His palm was up pushing toward me and I cut his palm in the meaty portion just below the thumb. We were both shocked, I was instantly disgusted with myself. The cut was only about two inches long but the skin separated instantly, there was no blood at first but the muscle pushed out all blue and purple separating the skin.

I learned two valuable lessons that day. Never ever pull a gun or a knife on someone unless you are defending yourself or your family, that includes play and training. Regardless of the reason, you will live with the consequences forever.

Second, the guy reported it as an accident, forgave me and we were friends for years. What if I had seriously hurt or even killed this person? Both of our lives could have been ruined for no real reason.

An instructor cutting himself purposefully to show his students everything will be ok is just ridiculous.

Forgive me for rambling again, but thanks for listening Moshe.

Best wishes to you, your family and all IKI staff and members.

*JD, Okeechobee Florida*

I had some guys from another style want to come in the gym and train with real knives. I declined but did watch his video. The "disarms" they practice look a lot like a cooperating uki that is flowing with the defender. Looked more like a rehearsed circus act than self defense. I can't believe people are grabbing the blades. Fingers come off like sausage links. Seems more like an ego thing to say you train with real blades.

I don't see any advantage to training with a real blade. I have a friend that was stabbed 6 times once in a fight and didn't even realize it until he went home to shower afterwards. because of the adrenaline, you don't feel the stab. He was lucky to live. if you don't feel the real blade then what's the point in training beside machismo.

*Chris Cromer, South Carolina, USA*

# Roots and Branches

### July 17, 2015, Israel

I enjoy gardening, I enjoy watching things grow. But it can be frustrating, not only does it take plants, flowers, and trees a long time to grow but initially you do not even see it, for before a tree can grow up it must first grow down.

In this day and age, we want results and we want them now. And if you can't give it to me I will go someplace else and buy it. The pressure is on. But that is not the way of nature, and the results will not stand the test of time.

A purchased diploma is just a piece of paper containing lies.

Many people come to me with demands for immediate rank recognition, whatever they did in their life until now, they feel, is justification enough for an automatic rank from IKI. My answer is always the same, no.

*Roots*

You can take a plant out of the ground and stick it someplace else. Initially it will look nice, beautiful leaves and flowers. But if the roots are not strong, if the plant does not "take root" it will soon wither and die, and all the beauty will be lost. The above ground beauty is fleeting.

As a child, I loved to take the avocado pits and watch them grow. But first came the roots, always the roots. It was a long time before anything began to show on top.

But a valuable lesson was learned. You must go deep before you can go high.

The rabbis say we should be like a tree with deep roots and not a tree where the branches are greater than the roots. For a tree with deep roots, all the winds in the world can come but the tree will not be toppled. But a tree with branches greater than the roots will fall with the first strong wind.

The lesson is clear.

When I was working for the Israeli Ministry of Education as a Krav Maga teacher and curriculum adviser, I was frustrated. I was frustrated that they did not see why I should be paid more than a 21-year-old who just completed his military service. Yes, he completed his three-week military Krav Maga course and was fully qualified by the IDF, but no, he was nowhere near me in terms of ability, understanding. He did not have my roots.

I attempted to explain that my thirty years of experience should mean a few more shekels per hour. But they did not buy it. The younger guys had the branches; the leaves, the flowers, i.e... the youth, the "look", the muscles. But I had the roots. The roots are not always visible to the naked eye.

Not everyone can see the roots right away. For some it takes time. But the roots are there and they make all the difference.

Compare this to the bass guitar in a rock band. The bass guitarist is rarely the most famous in the band; most people cannot even identify the bass line. But if you take out the bass its absence will be greatly felt and noticed. Without the bass, there is no rock and roll band.

We want to see our tree growing tall. We want to see leaves and flowers and fruit. The roots are boring, underground, and not visible. But strong roots are the key to everything.

Remember, many vegetables are roots. Asparagus, potatoes, carrots, what is visible on top is not important; it is what grows beneath the ground that sustains us. The root vegetable is the key.

Often, I receive inquiries from "martial artists" who spend a few years here, a few years there, some time with Krav Maga IKML and some time with Super Static Krav Maga. This is a person without roots, he is a wanderer. You cannot add up five girlfriends to equal one happy marriage.

Go to any job interview and show a resume that includes five jobs in eight years. The interviewer will surely ask you why you can't stay in one job for any length of time. Roots.

Roots are the foundation. Practice the basics well, again and again. This is the foundation for everything that will come letter, for the branches, the leaves, the flowers. And even when those blow away with the wind the solid foundation, the deep roots will allow the flowers to grow back again.

# Ranks, Titles, and Respect in Krav Maga

### July 18, 2015, Israel

I was asked about titles in Krav Maga. The Japanese are very particular about it. You do not want to confuse a *sensei* and a *sempai*, or a *soke* with a *shihan*.

That is not the case in Krav Maga.

If you happen to see the Prime Minister of Israel, Mr. Benjamin Netanyahu, feel free to yell out "Hey Bibi", he will smile back at you. Our president goes by Ruby and our minister of defense is Bugi. There is no disrespect intended, and none taken.

It is not one's title that brings one respect and it is not a matter of using a title to show respect.

A man can call you: "Sir" or: "Master", but still, have no respect for you at all; it is the actions that count. Titles, as we say in Arabic, are *"Haki fadi"*, Empty words.

My title?

His holiness, Grand master, Founder, Grand Puba, Lodge Leader, Sovereign of Israel, its surrounding territories and the world.

But you can call me Moshe.

In South America, students generally call me Maestro, Master, Professor; all nice, but the way one is treated is more important, far more important, than any title. Respect comes from actions.

I, certainly, appreciate the respect shown by these titles, but I do not stand on ceremony. Actions, not words, are what count.

Many of our students join us with titles in other styles. Please remember, those are "other styles". Do not expect me to call you Dr. Professor, Sir, Shihan, Soke, Sensei, Grand Master etc. I will call you Joe, Steve, whatever you like.

Years ago, I became friends with a woman who worked at a martial arts store. She said people would call up to place an order and get upset if she did not refer to them as Sensei, or Master. She said: "Excuse me, I am *not* your student, I do not need to call you by any of these titles."

There are titles that become part of one's name, such as Rabbi. But even then, if you did not meet the person as a rabbi, but as a customer at the bank, it would not be expected.

Remember, actions, not words.

Respect is shown by honest direct communication. Bearing a grudge secretly, speaking behind someone's back, taking actions that show another in a bad light; these are signs of disrespect, no matter what title you use to refer to the person.

If you respect someone, talk to them honestly. Treat them properly. Ask them what they need from you. Be transparent.

As my father used to say: labels are for bottles, not for people.

# Think Ahead

### July 19, 2015, Israel

Frequently I receive calls from people seeking self-defense training. And then, they ask me if it is "serious". Not really sure what kind of answer they expect. "No, we usually just sit around and watch comedies; if you want serious training, I would suggest my competitors".

And then comes the question: "Will I lose weight and get fit, I am looking for serious training."

Well, you have come to the wrong place. No, that is not what self-defense is about."

I frequently advise people, those who are truly interested in self-defense, to read certain books, and no, you will not get fit by reading those books.

Didn't you say you want self-defense training?

What if I took a minute to talk about home protection, awareness, car-safety and how to stay safe on the road? Am I wasting your time with my words, since you are not physically active at the moment?

Did you say you wanted a self-defense class? Because the fitness class is just down the road. The only self-defense benefit over there, is that you will be able to run faster, but remember you can't outrun a bullet and often, you do not even have time to turn around.

Remember, we are talking about self-defense.

I like to use an example that defines real, effective, self-defense, as compared to self-defense that is really nothing more than yet another fitness fad. (Whose goal by the way, have nothing to do with you, you are the victim who must be separated from his/her money).

A few years back, a Jerusalem man saved about 100 children. Was he Rambo? Was he a Grand Master? Was he a boxing champion? Did he have a 10th *dan* black belt? Was he a former football player or a former Mr. Universe?

No, he was an overweight, out of shape, slow moving, sluggish sort of man. He was a man who had never trained a day in his life and probably, could not name a single martial art other than "karate".

He was an ultra-orthodox Jew living in a secluded neighborhood of Jerusalem, away from secular newspapers, away from television or other foreign influences.

And yet, he saved more lives than you. Than who? Than you, the reader. I doubt that many of you can claim to have saved over 100 lives, but this man did, without a single day of training.

How did he do it? By using what some consider a waste of time, using his thinking cap. (or maybe his thinking yarmulke)

I stress awareness, avoidance, proper clothing for travel etc., but what do people actually hear.... *He is talking and wasting our time, we came to train!!*

Did you? Or did you come to learn how to survive. What if I spent the entire lesson teaching you how to survive, but you did not lose any weight or break a sweat? Would it have been a waste of time?

Well, that depends, did you come to learn self-defense or to lose weight and "get fit". (Commercial style "Krav Maga")

This out of shape man, this man who never stepped foot in a gym was conditioned by the Israeli/Jewish mindset which I teach: He saw a man who looked "out of place", (yes, we do profile, because it works and saves lives). He saw a man looking around and looking hesitant. He watched him closely.

He saw an Arab carefully insert a large package into a trash can, right outside a school where over 100 students were enjoying their recess. He alerted the police. They dismantled a bomb that had enough power to kill all those children.

This man is a hero. Are you?

So, I am really impressed with your six pack abs that you proudly display at every opportunity. And I am really impressed that you entered a ring and for some reason clobbered another human being unconscious. And I am really impressed that you can do more push-ups than me, but can you save a human life?

Have you trained yourself to be alert and aware? Are you trained in real self-defense? That is what we at IKI Krav

Maga are all about. And sometimes we stop the physical part and we talk. And that talk saves lives.

So, next time you think about your workout time and how you want to spend it, ask yourself this: is it all about how you look? Is it about measuring your biceps or your hips? Or is it about knowing how to survive a shit-hits-the-fan, back to the wall, holy crap we are facing terrorist situation?

For that is our reality.

Come and train with us in Israel.

So, sometimes, it is not about fitness, it is about learning to think ahead, to understand the dangers and know what to look for. That Jerusalem man, cut off from modern secular society, knew what to look for, he knew the Israeli reality, and he became a hero.

He saved lives.

What would you have done??

# Charred Remains
### July 21, 2015, Israel

HI Tech merged with low Tech taught us, here in Israel, something amazing.

*A small, seemingly unremarkable burned parchment fragment found 45 years ago, during excavations on the western shore of the Dead Sea, has emerged after hi-tech sequencing as part of the Book of Leviticus from a 1,500-year-old Torah scroll.* (The Jerusalem Post, July 21, 2015)

At Ein Gedi, עֵין גֶּדִי not far from where I live, a parchment was found inside the holy ark, (where we keep our Torah scrolls). Now we know it was the remains of the third of the five books of Moses.

We know about the town of Ein Gedi since Biblical days, The Song of Songs speaks of the "vineyards of En Gedi" and today, again, a Jewish community lives there.

*According to Dr. Sefi Porath, Ein Gedi — a Jewish village in the Byzantine period during the 4th-7th centuries CE — was once a prosperous community that housed a synagogue featuring a mosaic floor and ark.*

> "The settlement was completely burned to the ground, and none of its inhabitants ever returned to reside there again, or to pick through the ruins in order to salvage valuable property," - he explained. "In the archaeological excavations of the burnt synagogue, in addition to the charred scroll

> *fragments, we found a bronze seven-branched menorah, the community's money box containing 3,500 coins, glass and ceramic oil lamps, and vessels that held perfume."*

The cause of the fire is officially "unknown" but logical speculation tells us that the likely cause of destruction ranges from Bedouin raiders coming from east of the Dead Sea, to conflicts with the Byzantine government.

Either way, we see here an ancient Jewish community destroyed by either Arabs or Christians. Is there anything new? Has anything changed?

For the archaeologists, this is a very exciting find, as it is for all of us.

> *The burnt relic is the most ancient scroll from the five books of Moses to be found since the Dead Sea scrolls, most of which are ascribed to the end of the Second Temple period - he said.*

Even the history that only now is coming out, the one being deciphered by Hi Tech along with archaeology, reveals a tragic event; a beautiful community burnt to the ground, synagogue and holy books burnt, and the heart cries out: how long?

So we fight back, and no, I see no need to apologize, not to anyone. My book: "Israel, A Nation of Warriors", I am told it is "controversial", it may "offend some people", I should expect some harsh reactions. Read my lips: I don't care!

For those whose holy ark was burnt to the ground 1,500 years ago, in Ein Gedi and for those who were murdered in the Farhud of the Muslim countries, and for those murdered by the Crusaders in the Christian countries, and for David and Bella Bielski murdered in Belarus by the Nazis and their helpers, for my great grandfathers' ten siblings and elderly mother who were sent to Auschwitz and never came back, for all of them I say, enough, we fight back.

But what else does it tell us?

Jewish history, a glorious history, but one filled with sadness. I have history books of the Jews from every land, and other than the book about the Jews of China, they all end in tragedy. The Chinese Jews succumbed to assimilation and natural disasters, the American Jews suffered more Antisemitism than anyone today cares to admit or discuss, the Jews of all the other lands ended up either having their throats slit, shot in ravines or gassed.

Today the Jews of France are fleeing. The Arab world is nearly devoid of Jewish communities. Even the handful of Jews left in Yemen are in grave danger.

So here we find a fascinating archaeological find that teaches us about a Jewish community here in our own land, the land of Israel, which was burnt, destroyed, the survivors fled and never even return to collect the money that was in the synagogue treasury.

What shall we say and what can be spoken?

You want to know why we fire back at the terrorists in Gaza while the UN/US condemns us? You want to know why we profile? You want to know why we are not Politically Correct and soft and cuddly people? Learn our history!

Our hearts break to see the young ones go to war. Even today a young boy of 18, another Moshe, a student of mine who I had Shabbat dinner with just two weeks, is now enlisting, and now his mother shares the panic of all Israeli mothers. But what choice do we have?

I do not want some archaeologist 1,500 years from now to find, Heaven-forbid, the charred remains of our community. No, and therefore we fight back, as a nation and as a community. We fight back not because we love fighting, but because we wish to survive. And that my friends, is the crux of this "conflict"; they want us dead and we choose life. Thus we are at odds.

And so we fight on, for as long as it takes, there is no end in sight. Peace is an illusion.

And may we achieve the Biblical words of "and the land rested for forty years."

I would be happy with forty days of quiet.

# Martial Arts Ornamentation

JULY 22, 2015, ISRAEL

History. Some people love studying history, while others find it boring and irrelevant. Well, say what you will, but it is always relevant. The old saying...those who forget history are destined to repeat it. The Russian winter crippled Napoleon and Hitler made the same mistake. History.

Study the history of nations, of empires, their rise and fall. Who disappears and who remains, and why. Trees that stood a thousand years suddenly shall fall.

Look at Rome, look at the United States of America, look at the Holy Roman Empire, the Byzantine Empire, the Ottoman Empire, you will see patterns. Yes, the unbelievable can happen. Where is the USSR? Defeated without a bullet.

Study history.

I am not an architect and I have never really had any great interest in architecture. Of course, on my trips to Europe; to Russia, Rome, Germany, it is always interesting to see the different styles of buildings, but I am certainly not an expert. I fail to pick up on the historical nuances that are hidden in architecture.

**Time out** - The siren is going. Thank God, it is only a drill. A Nation of Warriors must always be prepared for war. At this very moment, school children are being led by their teachers to the bomb shelters. We are ready.

Back to work.

In 1939, Albert Speer was having dinner with fellow artists in Paris. Please do not ask who Albert Speer was (March 19, 1905 – September 1, 1981), it is a name you should know. So Speer was having dinner in Paris at a place called Maxims'. He was discussing the history of art and architecture.

He discussed the new style that had emerged with the French Revolution - "Even its simplest furniture was beautifully proportioned"

"This style, I argued, had found its purest expression in the architectural designs of Boullée." (Inside the Third Reich, page 159)

Étienne-Louis Boullée (February 12, 1728 – February 4, 1799) was a visionary French, neoclassical architect whose work greatly influenced contemporary architects.

Speer continues to argue that as France became more powerful, the style of architecture became more and more elaborate, to the extreme. Sounds like Bruce Lee describing the evolution of martial arts into what it became in his day, a "classical mess".

Speer continues his analysis: *"elaborate ornamentation had been lavished upon the still classical basic forms until, at the end, Late Empire had achieved a resplendence and wealth that could scarcely be surpassed."*

But then he adds something amazing: *"Within it were revealed signs of decay which were a forecast of the end of the Napoleonic era."*

This troubled him greatly, years later. As he sat in the Spandau Prison for close to twenty years, he had ample time to think it over. He then realized that Hitler's' architectural designs were clearly signs of events to come; only he had not thought this out in time. He had not seen the writing on the wall, pride comes before a fall.

*"Had I been able to think the matter out consistently, I ought to have argued further that my designs for Hitler were following the pattern of the Late Empire and forecasting the end of the regime; that, therefore, Hitler's' downfall could be deduced from these very designs."*

And then he adds something quite brilliant: *"Probably only posterity beholds the symptoms of downfall in such creations."*

Now, do we all see the lesson here?

As Bruce Lee pointed out, martial arts, all styles, tend to get more and more elaborate. Artists like art. I am told that it takes thirty years to master Ninjitsu, but yet, in the days of Ninjitsu, the average life span of a Japanese man was only about thirty years. So, something here does not make sense. Over the years' ornamentation made the art more complex and the process of mastering it required more and more time.

The over ornamentation, as Speer pointed out, is the sign of decay. Getting too fancy = getting to be useless.

As Bruce Lee said, our goal is "simply to simplify", at IKI Krav Maga we share that goal. Each year our techniques become more simplified and more streamlined. Each year we make our style easier to learn, and more effective. Teachers, like artists, like to add, and add and add, but we believe less is more.

Keep it simple, keep it real, and keep it effective.

# Old Teachers

July 23, 2015, Israel

I recently saw a posting by one of our IKI instructors, a photo of his first instructors' tombstone/grave/ final resting place. He was speaking of his debt to his first martial arts instructor.

I was very touched. This is how it should be.

In our fast-paced world, where everyone wants instant gratification, we see people changing instructors like they change tires. There are new Krav Maga associations popping up every day and people fall prey to the "channel switching syndrome", i.e. with so many channels to choose from, people cannot stay with one channel long enough to actually enjoy a program.

There is an old and true saying; a jack of all trades, a master of none. Very simply this means that if you do not devote yourself to one art, you will never be a master of anything.

In Judaism we speak of how being a student is much more than accumulation of facts. We say that one should hang out with his teacher and pick up the little details of the teachers' life. There are great lessons outside the classroom, great lessons outside the books.

In Florida we opened a new IKI school with two wonderful instructors, Carrie and Scott. I was so delighted that our veteran instructors in that region showed up to participate, help out and support the seminar. I was so happy to see John, Joe and Gary there, along with several of their students. What a great family we have.

But then Joe said something after class that meant a great deal. He said that with every seminar, every class, that he attends, he gets more of "my heart". To me that means he understands more of my essence and the essence of IKI Krav Maga.

My friends, that will make a difference in the way he teaches.

*With Joe Cayer, the late Dr. Day, and John Liptak, Florida, USA*

In Judaism we say there is no such thing as a "former" teacher. A teacher is for life. We say if one taught you only one sentence, you are obligated to treat him with the respect due to a teacher for the rest of your life. Think about that.

You cannot fire a teacher. You can move on if you need to, at some point in your life, but a teacher remains a teacher.

As I grow older, more and more of my teachers and role models have passed on to the other realm and are no longer among the living, but their words live on with me. Their teachings are part of my life and I pass this on to you.

Old teachers are still teachers, their words still guide us. I have never let go of any of my teachers. A true teacher is a gift.

Some of my teachers wrote books, those books are on my shelf. When I pull them out, I always proudly introduce the book with...my teacher wrote this book....

I think of the late Rabbi Jacob Wehl of blessed memory. His book is in my library, but I recall vividly the days where it was not a book, but his actual presence in the class room. I was not reading his words from a printed page but I was hearing them with my own ears. And I still hear them..."Katz, mark my words, you will remember what I am telling you today, make no mistake about it..."

Ah...alas, for they are gone and none can be found to replace them.

The warm smile of Rabbi Wahrman of blessed memory, the quiet composition of Rabbi Heisler, the sweetness of Rabbi Laine. The passion of Rabbi Kahane and Rabbi Shlomo Carlebach. What teachers I have been privileged to have!

When a true student and a true teacher meet, both rejoice.

# Old Lessons

### July 23, 2015, Israel

We live in an era where new is good and old is bad. If you have a phone from the previous generation, i.e. a few months ago, you are passé, "out", some people will hardly be able to relate to you, let alone communicate with you.

I find that the term "old" descends upon us faster and faster each year. When I am told my computer is old, I respond with: "I have only had it a few years, how can it be old?"

An old book is a book written a hundred years ago, or at least a generation ago, an old movie is from the 1950's.

But old lessons, they still retain their value, their relevance, their crispness. We must never forget them.

At the end of the day, as I lay my troubled head down on the pillow, I say the same words that my mother taught me as soon as I was old enough to barely speak. Yes, the same exact words. Before I cross the street, I remember the words I learned as a child: "Look both ways before you cross", as I drive I can my mother saying to my late father: "Not you!! Keep your eyes on the road, I am pointing out the sites to the children. Focus on the road."

To this day I cannot look to the side as I drive, focus on the road.

And these words, these lessons, along with many others, have kept me alive to this day.

Let's think about that for a minute, shall we?

The common-sense lessons I learned as a child have saved me far more than any Karate or Jujitsu technique. My brain has saved me far more times than my body. But what happens in class? What happens in martial arts training?

We are all looking for the physical. Heaven forbid, you should interrupt the hard-core training to discuss self-defense, and, an uproar: "you are ruining my rhythm, my heart rate is going down, I came to train damn it!"

Looking both ways before crossing the street has saved me many times from being hit by a car. Looking both ways before making a decision in my life has saved me from great trouble, headache, and expense. When I violated this rule I paid dearly.

Look both ways before you make a decision, what will be the ramifications and results of this hastily made decision or promise?

Let's face it, using our brains before using our bodies, is the intelligent way to defend ourselves, as Mr. Miyagi said: *"Best defense, not be there"*.

Yes, those old guys had some good wisdom tips. The tough training guy looked pretty cool, but the old wisdom won out in the end, as it always does.

Sometimes it is the soft spoken one who has the most to say. Sometimes words are more powerful than actions. This is not an alternate to physical training; do not misunderstand my point here. But mindless training will not prepare you for battle. Infantry without maps, cameras, spies, and intelligence will not succeed. More men were saved by the genius Alan Turing who was behind breaking the Enigma code in World War Two, than by the toughest, bravest combat soldier.

So sometimes stop and think, before you act or train. Look both ways before crossing the street. No matter how well built you are, no matter how strong you are, you are still not stronger or faster than the oncoming bus.

Think about it.

Sometimes, a random word of advice, a hug by a stranger, a smile by a child, a song, or ...a blog, can make the difference in our lives, can give us the strength to move forward.

# Sports Self Defense

AUGUST 2, 2015, DURBAN, SOUTH AFRICA

Sports skills take years to develop. If you wish to be a star baseball player, you will have to train hours a day. You will have to perfect your swing, learn to run after fly balls and dive to catch line drives.

If you wish to be a star hockey player, you will spend hours and hours on the ice and do endless drills. That is the price to be an athlete. It is not for everyone.

The same is true of sports martial arts. To be a champion MMA fighter or BJJ, wrestler, whatever, it will take serious training. You will have to train to compete against other athletes hell bent on winning. It will take some serious devotion.

My problem is when people try to apply this to real self-defense situations. There is really almost nothing in common between sport martial arts and real self-defense.

The skill-sets that sports martial artists have developed, are not relevant for most people. Krav Maga is for "most people", not only for top athletes in the prime of their lives.

Sports martial arts depend upon anticipating attacks, being ready and being in ideal situations such as on a mat or in ring. None of this has anything to do with a real violent confrontation.

Applying techniques that were perfected in the ring to real-life violent situations is impossible and highly dangerous. All the circumstances are different. 'Ready' is replaced by 'surprise', 'prepared' is replaced by 'exhausted', in proper sports 'attire' is replaced by a business suit, young and fit is replaced by any age and any level of fitness. You are not in the gym; you are walking home after a long day of work. The last thing you are ready for, is a fight.

And yet, I constantly see sports techniques being applied to self-defense. I say the entire starting point is totally different. These are two totally different fields of expertise.

I have trained in both, for decades, and have come to realize that mentally and physically they are totally at odds. The mindset that it takes to succeed in one, is irrelevant to the other. They have little in common.

I recall when the great basketball star, Michael Jordan, tried his hand at baseball; I admire him for this courage. As you may recall, he was a total failure. I greatly respect him for not being the Star, but being humble and giving it his best shot. He tried something new, and he tried it in front of the camera with the world watching. Baseball and basketball are different. The ring and the home/street are different.

Please, do not get them confused.

With sports fighting you are watching your opponent, you are observing patterns of movement, of attack. You are dancing around the ring and are in a "relationship" with the other fighter, as Bruce Lee would say. You are playing a game and looking for openings. You are mentally prepared, you have agreed to this fight, you knew ahead of time the time and place and opponent. None of this has anything to do with an armed assailant barging into your home in the middle of the night.

Please, do not get them confused.

# Fences and Krav Maga
### August 6, 2015, Johannesburg, South Africa

South Africa; no shortage of troubles. From load shedding, to police killings (55 so far this year), to plummeting currency rates and corruption, things are tough. People certainly have a lot to be concerned about. One of the greatest fears is home invasion crimes; break-ins that can turn violent.

So people build fences.

They build fences, high fences, with electrified barbed wire. They use bricks and metal and wire. They install security cameras and home security systems and they feel safe.

But are they?

Every-time I come here, I hear stories of home break-ins. No matter how high a wall they build, somehow the criminals find a way to get in, not all the time, not in every home but...all too often; Too often for the residents to feel comfortable.

Every visit I hear more horror stories.

And what happens then? Sometimes, members of the family have guns and they shoot, sometimes they have trained pit-bulls and they sic the dogs on them. But this is not a fool-proof solution.

While I was here, one young woman shot two security guards who came to investigate a "panic call". The young woman believed they were the criminals trying to break in.

Another woman sent her four pit bulls to attack two criminals, who again turned out to be the good guys. One of those security guards is in the hospital now recovering from his wounds. The other is facing charges for shooting the dog that mauled his partner.

Not a great situation; people are worried, very worried, and nervous.

But are they flocking to Krav Maga classes?

Are they trying to make themselves the human weapon, the last line of defense?

Are they preparing themselves to defend against a knife attack, a gun threat, a hostage situation?

On the whole, no, they are not.

At our recent seminar we did have a few, very few, people who had survived such a home invasion. By pure luck or Divine help, they emerged unharmed physically. Emotionally no one forgets such an experience.

The events happened to some of them years ago, when they were innocent teenagers. Now, years later, those events and images are still with them. They have taken this trauma and channelled it into Krav Maga training. That is a correct and healthy approach, but one that, sadly, few people take.

That is why I always say that I have great respect for anyone that walks into the Krav Maga training hall, by your action of just coming to class, you have already separated yourself from the masses, you have already shown yourself to be a doer rather than a viewer. If you come to Israel to train, you have certainly made a commitment, you have certainly invested in your own personal security. You have proven you are serious about your personal safety and that of your family.

We try our best to build good fences. We try to get good guns. But a time will come when it will be you, only you, no walls, no fence, no alarm, no gun, no knife. And you must ask yourself; when it is your life and the life of your family on the line, will you be ready?

# Clear Language
### AUGUST 8, 2015, SOUTH AFRICA

Language; All creatures have it. In Africa I observed animals in the wild. It is clear that they communicate and communicate clearly. If only we humans could learn a thing or two from them.

In each group there is a hierarchy where each individual knows his and her place. No one is demanding equal rights; that is not the way of nature. Equal does not work the way we want it to.

If you are not suited to lead, then you must not lead. You do not deserve your "share" of leadership. If you do not have medical knowledge, then you do not have the right to be head of a hospital. This is the way of nature.

So the animals communicate. Where there is danger, when there is a need to move on to greener pastures, when it is mating season, they communicate and they understand each other. There is order in their lives.

We too need to communicate in order to preserve order, in order to avoid and resolve conflict.

There was an issue between two of our instructors recently. They got together over lunch and the entire issue was resolved. That is how two mature men resolve an issue. They do not need a physical or legal fight.

We need to set rules and use language clearly. I learned the difficult way. For years I taught Krav Maga seminars at universities, colleges and high schools. At times problems would arise as a result of a lack of clear communication.

Are we booked?

The answer would come in various forms, *"We are so excited about hosting you at University of...."*

*"We can't wait for our students to meet you".*

*"We look forward to a great experience".*

But as I was double and triple checking and confirming, (Yes, that is the way I am). I would be told... *"Sadly we are not able to host you this year."* or various other phrases along those lines.

But I thought we were confirmed?!?

I learned my lesson. From that point onward when I would receive a "looking forward to seeing you on our campus" I would reply with: Answer me in the following format, anything less and I will consider the event not happening. I need to hear from you the following words:

"Yes, Moshe, we are confirmed! We will be hosting your Krav Maga seminar on this date. The event is guaranteed and you will be paid. This is our formal confirmation."

Now we are booked. I learned that vague language counts for nothing. I demand clear answers or there is no deal.

This has improved my life and reduced stress. Clear simple language has improved my quality of life.

*Rules*

Part of good communication and good business is establishing rules. Who pays for the seminar? When must I book the flight? Where will I stay?

All this must be clearly outlined. There is a Jewish law that dates back to the Torah, the Bible. It is one that I have never been crazy about because sometimes I too feel the need to take the law into my own hands, but have learned to see the wisdom in it. **A person cannot judge a financial matter for himself.** This means you cannot decide that someone owes you money and therefore you are justified in taking money from him without his consent. I.e. you feel a store sold you damaged merchandise, you feel entitled to a replacement so you go and steal the item: This is not allowed.

You feel you are being underpaid at work, so you decide to make less effort. That is unacceptable.

You must present your case to the proper authorities and then they can decide if you in fact deserve compensation. You cannot be the judge of your own case. You cannot say I feel entitled to take a little more. Sadly, you must work within the system and respect the rules of the place. I say "Sadly" because I too feel frustrated sometimes and feel like I am entitled to go to your bank account and take what I deserve.

When we host our Tour and Train program we too must follow the rules. I have brought many groups to *Masada* and yet I still must pay for myself each and every time. I personally feel that by now I should be allowed in for free, but the rules are made by the host. Their rules are that if I bring thirty participants I can enter without paying. In our recent Tour and Train we had 21, I had to pay. The guest does not make the rules. I cannot attend and then decide I am not paying.

Allow me to share a personal story, one that you can learn from. I know I have.

*Shuki, me and Yad Vashem*

Yad Va Shem Holocaust Memorial is a very visited place. As such it is wise to control the number of people who visit each day. Therefore, if you are a group leader you must book in advance and receive approval to visit on any particular day.

Fair enough. Makes sense, you can't have 5 busloads of tourists and school children and soldiers all enter at the same time, you will not be able to move. To enhance the experience for everyone the group visits must be coordinated in advance.

I came one year with a small group, seven participants. This hardly constituted a group by my definition. In fact our Bible defines a group as ten adults. So be it.

The "group manager" Shuki, spots me and stops me on the spot. He declares that we are a group and demands to see my reservation. I did not make a reservation.

I argue with him. I am terribly worried that my overseas guests will not be allowed to enter. It gets loud and nasty. I insist that seven is not a group but Shuki tells me that as

Yad Va Shem group manager he and he alone shall decide what constitutes a group and what does not.

He is correct. I am wrong. Yes, that happens now and then.

Eventually I realize my only hope is to admit defeat, admit that I am wrong. No, I did not check the Yad Va Shem website, no I did not read the section on groups and no I am in no position to argue. So I admit my mistake, and plead my case asking for mercy. My group is allowed to enter but I am not.

I spent some time with Shuki. I get to know him a little. He really is a good guy and it was wrong of me to step on his toes and challenge his authority. This is his job and he takes pride in it, as he should.

From that point onward I followed the rules. I contacted Yad Va Shem beforehand, I filled out the forms, listing my name, address, phone number, size of group, purpose of visit, countries of origin etc...and faxed it in and waited for the reply.

Once I learned to follow the rules everything worked out fine and we always were able to visit on the day we wanted.

But there is more to this wonderful story. (at least I think it is wonderful).

Now when we visit Yad Va Shem I always make a point of going over to Shuki and saying hello. I introduce him to our group and say "Everyone say 'Hello Shuki'"

He loves it and smiles that wonderful smile of his.

But there is more.

First thing that I do when I enter the center is I go downstairs to the cafeteria and say "Coffee and cake for Shuki please, give me something he likes". I bring this to Shuki, he smiles and says, *"Ein camocha Moshe"*, there is no one like you Moshe.

We have become friends. And that my friends is the lesson for today. There is no greater victory that turning an adversary into a friend. And sometimes that involves admitting that we are wrong, that we misunderstood something. Sometimes we actually need to say, "Sorry, I was wrong".

And that might be difficult for some of us, but just think of the rewards!

Do you want to go down with a sinking ship and a sour face rather than admit you are wrong? or do you want to ask for forgiveness, work together and sail safely to shore?

The choice is ours.

# Train No Exit
### August 3 2015, Durban, South Africa

No one ever promised you an easy life. No one ever said it would be easy. You can be born in times of peace, but end up living your life in times of war. You can be born a prince, but live your life as a slave. You can be born into great wealth and privilege, but see all that go up in smoke and need to fend for yourself.

Life has its ups and downs, as the Dude says.... Strikes and gutters. Sometimes the downs seem so down, so painful, that we do not want to go on. We feel like shouting "Stop the world I want to get off."

But we cannot. We do not choose the date of our birth or the date of our death. We are born and die against our will, so teach the rabbis.

And now we must make the best of it because.... there is no exit!

As the old saying goes...this is the hand you are dealt and this is the hand you must play. Some of us are dealt a great hand and others are dealt a more "challenging hand".

I know of a man in Brooklyn, his name was Yehuda, bless his memory. I met him only briefly. He was labelled as "slow" or mentally handicapped. Sadly, his family felt he would not bring honor to the family, would hurt the chances of success for his many siblings. He was disowned and left to fend for himself.

A couple of years ago I heard that he died; Collapsed on the streets of Brooklyn, alone. But a great man is never truly alone.

His family abandoned him, was ashamed of him, until they learned more about him, after his death. Although his funeral was not publicized by the family, it was attended by hundreds.

The young handicapped man had become known as a *tzadik,* a righteous one. Living alone, he attended prayer services every morning in the synagogue. He was uneducated, but became self-taught. He fixed things, he drove a cab and he helped people.

If one did not have money: "That's OK" - he would say - "pay me when you can." He was a man of the street and he helped everyone. He knew loneliness and he understood pain. He helped everyone. He was eulogized as one would eulogize a great rabbi. He was the *rebbe* of the street.

Yehuda, of blessed memory, was not dealt a great hand in life, but he made it a great hand. He added to this world. And so can we.

I am in South Africa, teaching a series of Krav Maga seminars and I am hearing many stories. People have a great deal that they must cope with here, but they are finding solutions. There is no other way.

There is no exit until...that day comes. So, we must make the best of it, we must train hard, we must take the hands we were given and make them our winning cards.

You have no choice but to contend with this life. I saw a sign "No Exit" during one of our Krav Maga seminars in Durban, South Africa and I made this connection: As there is no exit, improve your chances by training in Krav Maga. Choose not to be a victim. Make a decision to improve your life, learn to protect yourself. There is no exit.

I recall the old story of *Solla Sollew*, (Dr. Seuss) where there never are troubles, or at least very few.

Solla Sollew is a tale told in the first person by a young narrator who experiences troubles in his life, mostly aggressive small animals that bite and sting, and wishes to escape them. He sets out for the city of Solla Sollew ("where they never have troubles / at least very few") and learns that he must face his problems instead of running away from them. He then goes back home to deal with his "troubles," arming himself with a big bat and resolving that "Now my troubles are going to have troubles with me!"

So we train in Krav Maga, so that our troubles will have trouble with us.

Our young hero learns that *"I learned there are troubles of more than one kind; Some come from ahead and some come from behind"*.

There is no exit. But we can make life better, one Krav Maga class at a time.

# A Soft Breeze Blows

August 10, 2015, Israel

Apparently I missed a great heat wave, my plants look terrible and everyone is feeling exhausted. I just returned from South Africa and the heat here has been severe. Such is life, we still thank God everyday for our great country and our freedom.

But the heat hits hard.

This morning I woke up, opened the windows and doors and a soft sweet delicate breeze entered my home. I felt renewed: Renewed as our nation is renewed.

Though times come and go, such is life. Every nation and every individual has his tough times. They say tough times never last but tough people do. In that case we must be a very tough people to have lasted this long.

But as the soft sweet breeze hit me a thought entered my mind; the after!

Everyone complains during the heat wave, everyone seeks relief and shelter but like the monkey who complains in the rain we do not build shelters afterwards.

Tragedy hits, we feel terrible for a few hours, and then we move on as if nothing happened. We leave it to the professionals to deal with crime, war, home invasions. We quickly return to our daily normal lives.

But not all of us.

It still boggles me that after all our people have been through there are still Jewish communities living abroad and oblivious to the dangers. For me the turning point came at a very early age, the formative years of first grade through seventh, when my fate became inextricably tied with my people and our land. The images of the Holocaust, the stories from survivors, the nightmares and the dreams lead me to where I am today and who I am today.

The phrase *Never Again* became our slogan, and as Rabbi Kahane explained it did not mean never again would there be a war against the Jews but never again would we be unprepared.

Never Again

But yet as the soft sweet breeze enters our home and our hearts after an oppressive heat...we forget. We forget and we return to normal daily life.

But not everyone forgets. During our counter terrorism training our instructors constantly bring up the past, the Holocaust, the Shoah. These Israeli born battles hardened warriors still think back, daily, hourly, on our horrific past.

As each group concludes their training our instructors talk about "what happened" and how "as long as I stand guard it will not happen again, you are safe."

We do not let the quiet times erase our memories. When the hard times are over we do not go play like carefree monkeys in the sun, we build, we plan, we train. We make sure "it" doesn't happen again, not on our watch. And we train the next generation to think the same way.

A soft delicate breeze touches our cheeks and reminds us of all the goodness in this world, it reminds us that after the heat wave there is that pleasant breeze. After the storm comes the calm. But we must not let it fool us; we must not forget that there is work to be done. We must not forget that we must prepare.

# Krav Maga Sparring

### August 11, 2015, Israel

The question comes up now and then; is there a place for sparring, or fighting in Krav Maga?

The answer is simple; yes and no.

When I see "Krav Maga competitions" or "Krav Maga tournaments" that is a sure sign that someone misunderstood what the term means. There can be no such thing as a Krav Maga competition.

Krav Maga is not a sport. It is not kickboxing, or Judo or MMA or anything along those lines.

Terrorists, muggers and rapists are not sportsmen. Rape is not a sport nor is hijacking.

The entire point of Krav Maga is pure self-defense and nothing else. The entire point is you will not be in the mood for a fight, you will not be looking for a fight and you will not be prepared to fight just now.

You will be out for dinner with your family, you will be waiting impatiently for the train or bus to arrive, you will be withdrawing cash from the ATM.

You will be wearing a business suit perhaps, a dress, a skirt, a winter coat, not a karate *gi* or Thai boxing shorts. You could be in an elevator, a narrow stairway, a small entrance to an apartment building, on a boat, on a goat, with a bat or a cat, at night with a kite, at day or at play...anywhere, anytime.

You will not choose the time of the event, you will not choose your partner.

So there is no sparring in Krav Maga. However...

Sparring does have its place as a supplement to Krav Maga and we should include it in our training, within limits.

**Pros and Cons:**

**Pros**: We must all learn to cope with fear and pain. We must all know what it is like to see a punch or a kick coming our way. We must feel some pain, perhaps even see some blood and keep on going. We must test our will to live, our will to survive.

Feeling a little fear, a little pain, is an important part of our Krav Maga training. Sparring gives us that opportunity, to feel fear and pain, to experience a little bit of a real confrontation.

**Cons**: Some people may develop "Sporting habits". We must remember that a kickboxing fight, or MMA style fight, is very different from a real attack.

We do not want to see our students rolling around on the ground looking for an arm-bar, or dancing around in circles trying to get that perfect roundhouse kick. We must remember that this is not a movie. The incident must be over in a matter of seconds.

**Conclusion**: Krav Maga is not a sport. It is an art of self-defense and survival. Getting home alive is your only trophy. Other activities can be great supplements to your

Krav Maga training such as sparring, general fitness, good nutrition and learning foreign languages.

# The Cobbler, Adam Sandler

August 13, 2015, Israel

I do not watch many movies but when I do, it is on an El Al flight. On a recent flight to South Africa, the lovely flight attendant recommended I watch "The Cobbler" with Adam Sandler. I am glad I took her up on it.

The movie begins in Yiddish, always a heart-warming sound, in the Lower East Side of New York, 1903. My family arrived there a little bit later. My grandmother was one of the first in her family to be born in America, in 1908. Her father and uncle owned "Levine Brothers' Hardware".

The scene brings back memories of my visits to the Lower East Side with my cousin Ephraim, retracing the footsteps of our early American immigrant families. I know they worked hard, lived on very little, spoke Yiddish and learned English.

Back to the movie.... After the initial scene in Yiddish, the movie jumps to current times, and Max Simkin (played by Adam Sandler), a Jew from Brooklyn is the fourth generation descendant of Pinchas Simkin who was in the 1903 scene.

Without going into the plot of the movie, Max is a simple guy, a good guy, a nice guy. The kind of guy that most women do not get overly excited about. He works in his fathers' shop, repairing shoes, making a very modest living and living at home with his elderly dear mother, whom he lovingly takes care.

He has Coke Cola with his lunch, coffee for his break, reads the Daily News and chats with his neighbor, Jimmy the barber.

Women come into this shop all the time but never take notice of Max... until a magical change takes place. Due to circumstances beyond this blog, Max discovers the ability to change bodies as he wears the shoes of different people. Soon he can experience what it is like to be white, black, Asian, female, etc. (there is no racism here whatsoever and just to be on the safe side, the main villain in the movie is a middle aged Jewish woman who controls a mob of blacks and Italians, very likely of course!).

As Max experiences living in other people's bodies, he has interesting encounters. In the body of a famous DJ (considered good looking by women) women come up to him at a bar and invite him over for the night. (which does not work out, because once he takes off his shoes, he is back to being Max).

But suddenly he is sought after, only because he looks different, but yet, the real Max, a good honest man from a good family, cannot get a date.

Alone and lonely, Max spends time with Jimmy during the day and with his dear mom during the evenings.

At the end of the movie, after getting to know Max through a bizarre series of circumstances, one of the local women finally realizes that all along she has been with a remarkable guy, a truly good guy. She finally appreciates what other women have overlooked. The movie ends as she invites him for dinner.

### *The moral of the story.*

So, how does all this fit in with Krav Maga? Real simple. Most of what I see today in the commercial Krav Maga world is like some of the characters played by Sandler, when he puts on their shoes: the cool guys, the Gangster types, the Pretty boy DJ that the women want for a quick relationship, all the shallow and worthless types. But Max, the real Max, the true Max, is just a decent sort of guy, the kind that most women these days overlook, the kind of guy who makes a good husband and father.

Max is a shoemaker in the Lower East Side. He is not a "Professional", he works with his hands at the same profession as his father Abraham, grandfather Hershel and great grandfather Pinchas. He is real. He works hard, provides a valuable service at a fair price. We all need shoes. But suddenly, being a shoemaker is not good enough for the women.

We all need self-defense. IKI Krav Maga is not flashy. We do not act like gangsters or pretty boys. We do not have Hollywood celebrities on our website. We do not train people to do Movie style Krav Maga.

Like Max we are simple, hardworking, real and really effective. In over thirty-five countries and in many police and military circles, our style has proven itself where it matters most, in the lives of real people.

# Find A Path
### AUGUST 14, 2015

Life is about finding a path. We need to find our way in the dark. We are born into this world without consent. We do not choose the time or place of our birth. We do not choose the religion we are born into, the family, the clan, nothing...

All men are created equal but none are born equal. Were you born as heir to the Czar or as a peasant with no hope? Where you born with the natural talents and gifts of a Mozart or are you one of the countless ordinary people that fill the earth?

The circumstances of our birth and early life are beyond our control. But eventually we must find our path in life. Like a trickle of water running down a rocky hill we must find that little opening, that little space that says... *Yes, you can squeeze though here.* Here you find your opening; here you find your path in life. That is how you start to make your way in life, to make a difference, for yourself and for others. You must believe that you deserve a life.

I wrote of my family on the Lower East Side, New York, USA at the early part of the century, (1908). I recall when visiting the museum of the Lower East Side seeing in one of the rooms a pair of boxing gloves and a pair of light weights. The tour guide explained that the young Jewish man who owned these was dreaming of becoming a boxer. Why a boxer? What kind of a profession is that for a man born to a family of rabbis? Because for that young man boxing was seen as a way out of the ghetto, out of the slums, out of the terrible poverty in which these poor immigrants lived. He was seeking his path, his way out.

Some turned to crime, others became peddlers and eventually became owners of huge chains of food stores and clothing stores (and now other people burn and trash these places and say, "why don't we own such stores", Why? because you are a goddamn lazy good-for-nothing living off of other people's work, that's why.)

So my family worked all day, eat little and went to the "School for New Americans" at night to learn English. The next generation all became professionals. No belly aching, only hard work, hard decent work.

Jews saved up and rented sewing machines, they worked around the clock, slowly buying their own machine, and slowly moving up the ladder of success. My grandfather Moe Katz sold materiel, my grandmother Mina Katz made dresses. They worked hard. They found their path among the rocks. The trickle of water came through.

Your path out might be a very narrow one but you must find it, just wide enough for the trickle of water, and then you expand and make it a highway.

With Krav Maga it is the same. No one promised you an easy life and you may face danger your entire life. So we look for the shortest possible solution. We look for the path to the target, the path to defend ourselves.

With a strike to the face we use a very simple natural and intuitive block. We drive forward and using the most narrow of paths we strike at the vulnerable points of the bastard who tried to hurt us. We have no time to waste.

This is not a sport. For the young man trying to fight his way out of the ghetto boxing was not a sport but a ticket out! At the time there were many Jewish boxers, not for the sport but for the ticket out. This was a painful way out but nonetheless an honorable way.

IKI Krav Maga is not designed for comfortable people. We do not have fancy elaborate techniques, we do not use artistic expression, we do not have time to play around, we are just looking for a way out of trouble. We need a short and direct path, simple.

We are seeking our path to freedom.

# Twenty-Five Years

August 15, 2015, Israel

For Shani

Twenty-five years ago, my niece was born. Twenty-Five years, that is a quarter of a century, a landmark.

When I returned to Israel in January 1990, my dear mother (may she live to 120 years) and my dear father of blessed memory, met me at the airport. My sister in law was pregnant with my niece, my first niece. I remember that moment.

Twenty-five years. What have I done with that time?

I had trained in the USA at the Kyokushin Oyama school of Karate. Among the Japanese that was known as the "real tough killer Karate". I chose it, because it was the most challenging school I could find in New York, I was not looking for the easy path.

In New York, I enrolled in college and asked my adviser for the most difficult program they had, yes, a little crazy perhaps.

So I was studying Finance and Economics, working on Wall Street, training at the Oyama dojo five days per week, at least and studying Talmud at the renowned Chaim Berlin Yeshiva. What full days I had.

My time at the Oyama dojo was well spent. I had the privilege of training each morning, after the regular class, with the *uchi deshi*, the apprentice instructors who came from Japan to train with our teacher. School of hard knocks.

When I returned to Israel I was looking for the same kind of school, I wanted the real deal, I wanted to pay my dues.

My friend Alon from Memphis, Tennessee, a former world champion power lifter, said the only place to go was Itay Gil. I took his advice, I spent the next eighteen years there. If you find something good; you stick with it.

Twenty-five years ago today, my niece was born, time to reflect on life. What the hell did I do with my time?

What I did is become a world expert in self-defense, why? Because I give a damn. Why? Because I am sick and tired of seeing good decent people living in fear. I have not solved the problem, but I have certainly contributed to the solution.

Twenty-five years. I studied karate, boxing, judo, Wing Chun Kung Fu, Brazilian Jujitsu, pressure points, Thai boxing and....much more.

I have not rested, I have not taken it easy.

I wrote a book, I wrote perhaps over a thousand blogs, articles, editorials. I have been interviewed all over the world. I've had a special segment about me on Slovak TV, featured newspaper articles. I am not saying this to boast, but to say I have given it my all to make a difference. The Karate Kid from the Los Angeles Jewish Defense League, has seen the world.

And I am not done, far from it.

My training comes from my pain, and from my love. Pain from our suffering, the endless suffering of the Jewish people, and love for all decent people. The pain never ends and the self-examination never ends.

Twenty-five years ago today, my niece was born and when a child is born we make a promise. I promise you that I will do all in my power to make this world a better place.

The world has become more dangerous, more brutal and more corrupt, but I keep my promise. When a child is born into this world, we look at their sweet innocent eyes and say...You have no idea what you have just been brought into, but I will do my best to make it a little safer, a little better.

I am keeping my promise.

Are you keeping yours?

# Beginners Luck
### August 17, 2015, Israel

Is there such a thing as luck in life, or do we create our own luck? Perhaps the "lucky" man works harder, or smarter, or has the knack, or the courage, to seize an opportunity.

The lucky girl realizes a man is a great catch and goes for it, while the "unlucky" girl sees only a loser with no hope and lets the very same man slip away. And then she whines: "Why aren't there any decent men out there!" There are, but you need to be "lucky" to notice them.

And then, there is the concept of "Beginners luck". Some people "rely" upon beginner's luck, but I think this is nonsense. Last night, I had some insight into beginner's luck. I believe it is the absence of stress created by trying too hard.

Sometimes we can be our own worst enemies; we stand in the way of our own success. We need to remove those obstacles which we create. Some beginners have not created obstacles.

***Daniel San, you beginners luck!"***

The classic film, the Karate Kid, with the late great Noriyuki "Pat" Morita and Ralph Macchio inspired a generation of martial artists and filled karate schools with new students.

In that film, one of the classic scenes finds Mr. Miyagi meditating, while trying to catch a fly with chopsticks. Daniel walked in and saw him.

Daniel asks: "Wouldn't a fly swatter be easier?"

**Mr. Miyagi**: Man who catch fly with chopsticks accomplish anything."

**Daniel**: Did you ever catch one?

**Mr. Miyagi**: Not yet.

**Daniel**: Could I try?

**Mr. Miyagi**: If wish.

Daniel picks up a pair of chopsticks and joins Mr. Miyagi in this activity and succeeds, to which Mr. Miagi said: "you beginner luck."

But was it beginners luck?

Flashback a few years, Krav Maga Tour and Train...a young woman, petite, wins our shooting competition. She hits five balloons while her tall and muscular boyfriend and other similar macho guys score a cool zero.

I ask our shooting instructor: "Did you see this coming?" He said: "Yes, it happens all the time. As soon as she hit the first balloon, I knew it would end this way."

He explained; the "tough guys" had something to prove, they had to win. Shooting well was part of their "manliness" but no one had any expectations of a cute, little, petite blonde. Once she hit the first shot, she already exceeded everyone's expectations. Now she certainly had nothing to prove.

Having nothing to prove, makes us more relaxed.

She was totally relaxed and was thinking: "Wow, this is so much fun". Fun?!? The guys were visibly stressed. I do not care what year it is, men are men and these men, in particular the boyfriend, simply had to be the better shot.

So, the more relaxed she became, the more tense they became. A relaxed person performs better.

Last night a new student came in, sweet little girl, petite, about 11 years old. We were working on defense when a handgun is touching your forehead. I developed a technique for this situation, which I like very much. It is different from other styles of Krav Maga. It involves stepping out of the line of fire immediately and using an down-up chopping motion on the attackers' arm.

I fully believe in this technique and those that have learned it properly believe in it as well. But some...have difficulties.

I have seen black belts, experienced instructors, struggle with this technique for months and, ultimately, reach the conclusion that "Moshe goofed on this one". So they either "improve upon it" or drop it.

That is a mistake.

I try to teach them, relax, flow, take it easy and you will see how this is an amazing technique, once you get it, you will swear by it. Trust me on this one. So, last night this little girl tries it for the first time and....perfect!

I told her she is doing it better than black belts. Perhaps she thought I was just being nice. I never flatter students just to be nice. She was doing it great.

Perhaps it was "beginners luck", but I do not believe in that. What is beginners luck? It is this feeling that you are free from expectations. No one is expecting you to do great your first lesson, you are free to make mistakes and no one will criticize you. This is a luxury not afforded more advanced students.

So nothing is expected of you, and you are totally relaxed, and bam...you did it perfectly. Those who get nervous put in too much effort, too much pressure and they perform badly. And then the corrections they receive, place even more stress. Bad cycle.

So, there is no beginners luck, there is just that Wu Wei, the effortless effort. When asked what is the difference between where I am now and where I was five years ago, I jokingly say I have become more Chinese. What I mean is I flow more, I am more relaxed, I use less effort in my Krav Maga techniques.

What we need to cultivate in the higher ranks is that same attitude as the beginner; to be the Child again. As Bruce Lee said, we go from Child to Man to Child.

Free yourself from ego, from stress and just allow the technique to happen.

We have a lot to learn from beginners.

With IKI, Krav Maga Beginners are always welcome, you are a breath of fresh air. As Mr. Miyagi said - "To make honey, young bee need young flower, not old prune."

COMMENTS, QUESTIONS

Very astute observations. I totally agree. Learned a long time ago that if you relax things work much better for you. I guess also being older, more tired and more experienced allows one to relax a bit. I also think that once one gets to the point where he/she is not afraid to mess up in front of students, instructors, friends, etc., many things become easier and work better. All pretty much the same concept you outline.

**Hal Herndon, GA, USA**


QUESTION/COMMENT

Mixed feelings here, for anyone that is in an actual fight, especially a serious one, it is impossible to relax, so yes it can be done in training, but no one will be relaxed in an actual attack, so then under this condition at half of your best will you be able to respond correctly with this technique, every time

MY RESPONSE: THAT IS NOT REALLY WHAT I MEANT.

Difficult to put into words. Tensing up ruins all the techniques. People train wrong, have bad habits, everything turns out wrong and incorrect. They never fully "get" the idea and thus never fully appreciate the techniques.

When you do not appreciate a technique, you can never do it well, because without confidence the technique will never be correctly executed.

Like the technique I am describing, gun touching the head, many have trouble with this at first because they try too hard and they ruin it. I do it totally relaxed and when I "mean it" I do it even faster and harder and it works amazing. I see the shock and pain on the opponent. I believe in this.

My tension, aggression, etc. does not tense up the technique but rather makes it work faster, more powerful.

Learning to do it relaxed makes it more effective and when you do it "for real" it is even more effective.

Take shooting for example, every shot must be relaxed but yet Counter Terrorists are certainly not relaxed when in combat. Contradiction? No. They train to shoot relaxed because if they force the trigger the shots will not be accurate, and accurate they must be or they will kill innocent civilians. So the situation can be not relaxed but the technique is relaxed.

The actual fight will not be relaxed of course but imagine tensing up with every punch?

The tense punch does not work. It is slow and weak.

That is why fighters always loosen up before a boxing match.

I hope this makes more sense.

The punch without tension is much faster and more powerful than the "forced" punch. This does not mean the fighter is relaxed and taking it easy during the fight.

When I am in a fight I flow. This is how I trained and it works. My "tension" does not cause me to tense up but to flow even more.

Moshe,


I never really looked at "beginners luck" in this way. It makes sense. Also, women actually make better shots than men. There are several studies that have proven this. One of the best snipers in Russian history was a woman. Lieutenant Pavlichenko, her total confirmed kills during World War II was 309, including 36 enemy snipers. Besides, she became an instructor and trained Soviet snipers until the war's end.

***Gary Brielmayer***

# Be True to Yourself, Keep Your Balance

### August 18, 2015, Israel

The words above, "Be true to yourself, keep your balance" and "Rise above it" come from a dear friend in the Netherlands. These words are true, wise and old, but we sometimes forget.

Life has a way of unbalancing us, of taking us away from our mission, our goals, our true self. People draw us into things we do not want to be a part of. Like being drawn into a foreign war, we lose our true home.

We must remain focused.

When we start chasing an annoying fly, we lose track of what it was we were doing, our important life work. We must remember who we are and what our purpose is. We must maintain our balance. The two are totally interconnected.

When we become distracted by a problem - we chase it, we try to force a solution and we go off-balance. We get upset, we waste time.

What my friend was saying was: "Trust yourself, trust your life works. Do not let a minor nuisance take you away from your important work, which I recognize and believe in. Do not fall down to the problem, rise above it."

And in the words of my dear friend Hal: "Keep doing what you are doing".

There will always be distractions. There will always be hecklers. There will always be those who seek to find fault in you, criticize, accuse and condemn. Move on!

Rabbi Kahane of blessed memory would say: "They are like dandruff" and would make a sweeping motion on his jacket shoulder, as if wiping away the dandruff. He was never distracted by the Hecklers.

And neither should we. Friends come and go, clients come and go. We must remain true to ourselves. We must not change to suit the needs of an individual friend or client. We must remain ourselves, for this is our mission in life. This is our gift.

Do not give them the power, keep the power with yourself.

*"First learn balance. Balance good, karate good, everything good. Balance bad, might as well pack up, go home."* - Mr. Miyagi, ***The Karate Kid***

# And Moses Spoke...

### August 20, 2015, Israel

When I was in Rabbinical College, Yeshiva, and I would write letters to my brother Michael he would say... "Moshe, do you realize all your letters from Israel begin like a sermon? It sounds like you are clearing your throat and saying.... Ahem...so...And Moses spoke unto the Children of Israel...

Can't you write a normal letter?"

I guess the name chosen for me had an effect. Named for my grandfather Moe and having the name of the great leader Moshe/Moses ...public speaking, public roles, activism and leadership, were in my blood and soul.

Life is a calling.

So we open the Torah, the Bible, and so often it begins with ...and Moses spoke to the Children of Israel saying.... etc.

Let's stop and think, Moses did a heck of a lot of talking!

Indeed he did, because he had a lot of lessons to teach, he had a lot to get across. So do I. So I speak and I write. (not to compare myself to the great Moses).

But Moses was frustrated, the Bible clearly records that. He was frustrated with his people and he spoke about this with his best friend, his confident, his therapist, God!

And so we continue today. We have a lot to say. We have a lot to teach. And as was our first leader, we too encounter frustration, is anyone listening??

My dear father suffered the same fate, he often felt he was "shovelling shit against the tide", people just do not listen. That is why 3,000 years later we are still reading the words of Moses, because we still have not gotten the full gist of what he was saying.

However...

The good news is that some of it has sunk it. Yes, not all, but some. We still have problems, lots of them. We still discriminate; we still behave badly, man to his fellow man, and man to woman. But imagine where we would be without those words.

The words of Moses, the words of the Bible have influenced your life in more ways than you can possibly know.

The civil rights movement was spearheaded by the descendants of Moses.

The labor unions were founded by descendants of Moses. The rights of women, children, fair pay, social justice, education for all, none of this was a given. Socialism, Communism, Capitalism...all stem from a desire to improve the lot of men...the descendants of Moses. Marx may have converted away from his religion, but its lessons were still embodied in his soul. He could not escape it. Think what you will of Communism but Marx had his heart in the correct place, he cared deeply about human suffering, the message of Moses.

So, after all his talking, "And Moses spoke..." ...someone was listening, and slowly the words have had an impact. We have a long way to go but we have come a long way.

So, I will keep on talking, and writing, and we shall keep on reading the words of Moses until we get it right.

It is our job to repair the world, to start the healing.

This is why I write....

# Truth or Not
### August 20, 2015, Israel

There are subjective truths. I think chocolate ice cream tastes best, you think it is vanilla.

There are disputes about history, did the Jews at Masada really commit mass suicide or not? As archaeologist, Yigael Yadin said: "There are things we will never know". In each scholarly journal, our historians and archaeologists will debate; who were the Essenes? What really happened at Masada? Did Josephus write the truth?

On these topics there can be a debate. And on these topics, we can acknowledge that, perhaps, we are wrong. After all, what if we were wrong about the Sadducees and the Essenes? Would anyone today be in danger?

Other than a few very passionate historians, I think we are all safe on that one.

But what about counter-terrorism? What about the correct choice of firearms or Krav Maga? What if we are wrong on that topic?

I am passionate about Krav Maga, actually that is not true. I am passionate about human beings. I want people to be safe. So, this is not about martial arts, this is not about Krav Maga and this is certainly not about an individual named Moshe Katz, who happens to be me.

This is about a six year old boy who moved to Israel and found out the world tried to destroy him. This is about a new immigrant to Israel who saw signs saying "Danger, Mine fields ahead!" because only a couple of months earlier, all the Arab nations attacked Israel with the aim of obliterating her. This is about a 7th grade boy whose education was interrupted, because on our holy day, our Arab neighbors attacked us with the goal of finishing what the Nazis started. This is about a young man who saw his brother go off to war. This is about an older man who sees his nephews go off to war. This is about caring.

So, I am passionate about self-defense, about people getting home safely. And on this, I cannot compromise.

Now, in polite conversation it is always: "Yes, you are correct as well, sure, you have a valid point." Certainly so in our own troubled times, where people live in fear of being labelled "Politically incorrect" or even worse "racist".

So, we cannot disagree with anyone. And so it is with styles and forms of martial arts, Krav Maga etc. No one can say anything negative. And seldom is heard a disparaging word...

All styles of Krav Maga are equally valid, all martial arts have something to offer, etc., etc., etc.

But what if you want to say the truth? What if saving people's lives is more important than "being nice at the discussion table"? What if you don't really give a damn about insulting people, because you are too concerned about saving their lives?

What do you do? Personally, I speak the truth.

On the pages of this website, the written word, I will *never* say a negative or insulting word about any martial arts style or instructor. I will not expose the poor and unqualified teachers, but in person?

In person, if you are my student, or if you come to me sincerely for advice, I will speak the truth, the whole truth and nothing but the truth. And when did that become a bad thing?

If I feel a style is worse than useless, I will say just that. Some "more polite" types, will raise an eyebrow and look at me as if to say: "Moshe! My goodness, I did not expect you to speak this way."

Really? What did you expect? for me to validate and endorse a style that I consider harmful, just so I can be seen as "so 2015" and so polite?

Not happening. I will do my best to refrain from openly insulting anyone or offending anyone, but I will speak the truth as I know it.

*As long as I shall live, I shall speak the truth,* (Jan Karski).

# Pride, Fall, and Modesty
### August 23, 2015

MMA, tough guys, even tougher girls, prancing about and shouting "I am the best!"

And then when people get turned off by their obnoxious arrogant behavior we hear. ..."I worked hard to get to where I am. Why is confidence looked down upon? Why must I put myself down?"

Well, you *cannot* put yourself down. You have such an exaggerated and inflated opinion of yourself that you could not act modest if you took acting lessons.

Now here is a lesson. Pride precedes the fall. No matter how great you think you are right now. No matter how high you have reached, you will fall. That is a fact that no one can dispute.

No singer stays at number one forever. No fighter remains world champion forever. While you are drinking your celebratory champagne, there is some young hungry kid in the ghetto destroying the heavy bag, and he is after your title! He is after your hide.

So listen up big shot MMA stars, no one is telling you not to be proud of your achievements. No one is suggesting that you must "put yourself down". Let's learn some English. Confidence and Arrogance are different words with different meanings. Modesty and self-deprecation are different words with different meanings. Learn the difference.

No one likes an arrogant person. Modesty is always in fashion.

Now hear ye, hear ye. We all grow old. Yes, I know that is bummer to even bring it up. Those six pack abs... going to lose them. You think you will work out like an animal when you are 55, think again. Life takes over. So if you base your "self-confidence" on your MMA achievements, your ring victories and your body...all these things shall pass. Guaranteed. But if you allow this to lead to confidence coupled with modesty, you will emerge a powerful person. These virtues shall not pass with time, they will only grow stronger.

Strength diminishes with the years but Wisdom can increase, although for most people it does not. Some grow old, few grow wise.

A young Bruce Lee found that an old Yip Man could still defeat him, blindfolded. He wised up fast.

Modesty looks good on you, at any age.

No one is telling you to "think less of yourself", in fact you should strive to think more of yourself, but don't base it on how many people you could beat up.

So for all the boxers, MMA champs, and "Tough guy Baaadd Ass" people...get over yourselves. Your time is limited.

Be more. And be something that lasts.

# Changes
August 23, 2015, Israel

Cha cha cha...changes..

As a young man, I was accused of being stubborn. Now I realize that I was simply determined, and ...I did not like being pushed around or told what to do. Just because I was small did not mean others could push me around. My determination has proven itself over time.

When I began my studies at Business school, to earn my MBA in Finance, I was told that more than 65% of all students drop out before completing their degree. I was working full-time. I was the national coordinator for a Zionist student movement. I was training five days per week at the Kyokushin dojo and studying part time at a rabbinical college in Brooklyn. I finished my degree. It took four years of night school, but I did it.

Stubborn, or determined?

Of the thousands of students who passed through the doors of Itay Gil's gym, none earned a 4th dan black belt, other than me. Stubborn or determined?

In 1973, when I was just a student in Junior high school our enemies attacked us on our holy day, Yom Kippur, the Day of Atonement. Our teacher asked us kids to write a composition - "Why do you think the Arabs are attacking us?"

I wrote my paper, I still hold those same exact views today. Stubborn or simply correct?

Today we have this idea that if you refuse to change, you are stubborn. But not all change is good. Wisdom is to understand when to change and when to hold tight to the truth.

The truth is I have changed, when necessary. I am not stubborn, I am determined to find the truth, but when I find the truth, I hold on to it stubbornly.

My martial arts training has changed to suit my reality. It was not easy. When the Karate Kid came out, I was all Daniel San and Mr. Miyagi, the mystique of Karate, Japan, the Oriental wisdom.

I still hold the martial arts of the Far East in the greatest respect. I respect all fighting systems that have proven themselves over time, from the Mongols to the Russians to the Japanese. But the nature of combat is always changing. You cannot fight World War Two with World War One methods and weapons.

I found that my training was lacking. It was too formal; it was difficult to see the end result, the actual self-defense. For a long time, I followed the masters with the greatest of faith believing that my training would result realistic self-defense.

It was a rude awakening to gradually face the truth; I was not able to defend myself. You can toe the line only for so long.

As a teacher, I would look myself in the mirror and ask; will this really work? Is this really good enough?

I changed the way I trained.

I am not big on changes. I do not look for the latest style, (heck no!) or the latest phone or computer or car. I like the same old stuff. But when it comes to saving lives...our way, the Israeli way, is pure innovation. We must always be one step ahead.

We adapt, we survive.

So I trained for more than 3 decades. I studied fear, body movements, natural reactions. I studied street violence and analyzed terrorist attacks. I took the principles, I was trained with and developed them a step or two further. I believe Krav Maga is for everyone, not only for IDF soldiers from 18 to 21 years of age. Krav Maga is not only for super athletes.

Together with our team, here in Israel and around the world, we continue to test everything. The ultimate test is our survival and our techniques have proven themselves when it has been a matter of life and death.

Change. Do not try to sell me a new style of shoes or jeans, no thanks, I am wearing the same kind of stuff since the 1980's, but when it comes to Krav Maga, self-defense, survival, we make the necessary changes.

And yes...IKI has become a world leader in Krav Maga, and we ain't done yet.

# Can't Buy Me Experience
### August 24, 2015

Growing up as a fan of the greatest band in history, the Beatles, "Can't Buy Me Love" was regular airplay. You hear that often enough and the message sinks in. *"Can't buy me love, everybody tells me so"*.

Love is not about material benefits; marriage is not only a contract, an exchange of goods and services, at least not in our day. We believe that love should be something special, something that grows and develops over time. Professional skills should be viewed the same way.

In the old days, you began as an apprentice. You did not just take a course and start to work. You carried the tools of the master craftsman, you watched him, you did as he said and you learned a trade. You could not just buy a diploma on line. Can't buy me love, can't buy me experience, and can't buy me skills.

Experience and skill can only be gained by .... experience. Should be obvious. You work hard and you gain experience.

The same is true of any wisdom. The Talmud teachers that just as the disciple must study the texts, he must also "hang out" with his teachers, to pick up their "causal talk" for even in their causal talk there is great wisdom.

Remember one of the early scenes in the film "Karate Kid" when Mr. Miyagi sees Daniel learning karate from a book.... he makes a face and a comment with a clear message, you cannot learn martial arts from a book, you must have a live teacher. You must have a relationship with your teacher.

And there is no substitute for experience. And yet...many "masters" turn to us at IKI and want to have their previous ranks, somehow, magically transformed into equal ranks in our system. Offers of business and money come along with this. Sadly nearly all Krav Maga systems today, will gladly accept such people and the business that they bring. I have seen this happen again and again, I turn someone down, he joins another association and the very next day the new member is already listed on the company site as an Instructor. I call it the "company site" because I see these more as a business than an actual center of learning.

*"Tell me that you want the kind of thing that money just can't buy"*

Like the Beatles, we seek the real thing. You cannot buy your IKI rank, no, no, no... No!

The International Scene: Seminars, On line Training, DVDs

The world has gone international. In the past, if you wanted to train in a martial art not practiced in your country, you had to travel to another land and spend many years there. Today we have greater technology which provides us with greater opportunities. And yet, we must use them cautiously.

At IKI we do provide Krav Maga instructional DVDs and on line training. But is that enough?

That depends on the person. Everyone learns differently. We do not view these "distance" programs as our entire training program. We encourage our students to come train with us here in Israel and we provide an affordable way to do this.

I personally travel all over the world and offer seminars. It is the job of the student, beginner or instructor, to make every effort to attend those seminars. Take off time from work, do what you must, but be there!

The video clips are great, but there is nothing compared to in person experience. So we strongly encourage you to join us for Tour and Train in Israel, we strongly advise you to attend every seminar you can, that is offered by your teacher when he comes to your country or to a nearby country. This is your chance to ask direct questions, this is a chance for your teacher to observe you in person. This is a chance for you to gain that experience that you so desperately need.

I have yet to find a situation where I showed up and observed one of our instructors and said...This was a wasted trip, the guy knows it all, I have nothing to teach him. That has never happened and I imagine it never will. Learning never ends.

Experience, you can't buy it and yet, you truly need it. If you wish to become a master in your field, it will take blood, sweat and tears, i.e. experience.

# The Nature of Evil

### August 25, 2015, Israel

There are those who have experienced it first hand, there are those who have studied it, there are those who spent time "in the can", some have seen war.

Evil, it goes by many names, it walks in many ways, but it is always the same, it is always Evil. Evil sleeps beside you. Evil is all around us....

Keep looking because Evil walks behind you and certainly, Evil talks around you.

But what is the nature of evil? Can anyone know?

The only part about evil that concerns me is how to fight it off, better yet - how to be prepared. The root causes of evil I will leave to the psychologists, the sociologists, the anthropologists, the criminologists, the cryptologists and all your what have you.

*There's bad poison runnin' thru your veins*

People say you can't understand the crime in South Africa, because you are not a native South African, you cannot understand Arab violence, because you do not live in the Middle East. That is all true, partially. But it is not geography.

Evil comes in a million forms. You have your serial killer, your Christian Crusader, your Muslim Jihadist, your rapist, your home invader/family killer, your school shooter, your racist, your anarchist, your sociopath, your suicidal maniacs, Stalin, Hitler, those crazy guys in Asia... Need I continue?

They are all on the highway to hell, not on the stairway to heaven.

We do not need to understand the nature of each individual violent person or type, that would take too many lifetimes. We do need to understand hatred, true evil. You need to go deep into your heart and visualize, feel it, feel the hatred, feel the fear and then, apply it to your training.

I have seen it myself, a crowd of Arabs with blood in their eyes shouting: *"Itbach el Yahud"* Kill the Jew, Kill Kill Kill!!!! You feel it, and you never forget it.

So, whether it is a guy who can enter a home, kill every member of the family just to steal a few dollars, or a maniacal religious person...I say it is the same. It is a loss of respect for human life. Killing a person is no different than cleaning a toilet, just a dirty job to be done.

You have to feel it, you have to feel it in your veins, you have to make it real. People say to me you don't know what it is like in..... whatever country.

Well, in peaceful Norway, a guy shot up a bunch of kids, is there a unique Norwegian violence, I say not. Evil is evil.

Think of the worse and hopefully, you will not be surprised. Expect the worse; always be on guard and train!

Yes, when you arrive in a new country, you must study the nature of violence. The first thing I do is speak to the people. I want to know where the crime takes place and why.

Is it mostly gang violence? Is it directed against "rich" tourists? Is it religious or ethnic in nature? When does it usually take place, and where?

I want to know what to look out for, what places or times of day to avoid. But in terms of the nature of violence, that never changes. Expect evil, expect guns pointed at the head, expect knives flying in all directions.

Evil is evil. And you do not have to go far to understand it. Start by going deep inside yourself. Remember...evil sleeps beside you...

# Stories from Life, Krav Maga Works

### August 26, 2015, from around the world

But does it work?

This is the question we get asked all the time. Sometimes I am amazed by the questions. You spend your life doing something of value and then someone looks at you, "C'mon...but in a real situation you would never be able to pull this off."

Great words from people who have never trained and never tried. It is like saying to a rabbi or a priest, "Do you really believe there is some magical force listening to your prayers? C'mon, we are all adults."

My answer is always the same; you can only improve your chances by trying. When people ask me, "Hey Moshe, how many bad guys can you take out at once?" Well I know they have been watching too many cartoons. I do not waste my time with such people. They need help.

Over my many years of teaching I have not only heard many success stories from my own students, but even more gratifying are the many stories I have heard about students of my students. This means that my students, the IKI instructors, are passing on the information in a reliable way.

I wish I had kept a record of these stories, but I have not, below are just a few stories, some as I recall them being told to me, some in the words of the instructors who passed on the stories to me. There are many more success stories that have never been reported.

The main thing is our system, IKI Krav Maga, has helped many people, physically and emotionally.

*"Name withheld" is a little embarrassed about this but she told me that she used Krav when in Italy on her own. Anyhow some guy she was talking to suddenly wanted to kiss her and got really grabby and aggressive. She said she had to actually meditate later to figure out what she did but it was as follows: Throat strike followed by elbow strike to head followed by knee strike and then an arm-bar. Then she left him to his misery. Having seen her in some of our very intense multiple attacker scenarios in class, my guess is that the whole thing took somewhere around 2 to 4 seconds. She said it was a blur.*

*Anyhow, while none of us who are serious about self defense actually promote violence it is extremely rewarding to me that in just over 6 months she has developed the instincts and talents to handle the situation in a foreign land with foreign people and no backup without even thinking or planning what to do. Maybe it's self-serving but even though Jamie and some of the others have used what we've taught them "out there", this girl is not a fighter and doesn't put herself 'on the line' on a daily basis so I am very proud that it all worked. Of course, I must also offer my thanks to you for teaching me what and how to teach her.*

**Hal Herndon, Georgia Mountain Krav Maga**

Nicolo, an Italian who came to work with the "oppressed" so called Palestinians, began to feel threatened by the people he came to rescue. He began attending Krav Maga classes with me. One Sunday night we worked on being grabbed by the neck and pushed against the wall. That Tuesday he had a chance to use it.

Three Arab men attacked him outside the Old City walls. One grabbed him by the neck and pushed him against the wall. Nicolo said he could smell the beer and vodka on his breath. Nicolo used the technique he just learned and smashed the guy into the wall, causing instant bleeding. The other two brave warriors ran for the hills.

Yonat brought a friend to class. She stayed for only a few lessons. The reason she came was a sad one, marital violence. Soon I received a phone call from Yonat; good news and bad news. The good news is our Krav Maga works, the bad news the women's husband attacked her.

She decided to give the marriage a second chance and invited her husband back home. He attacked her and pinned her to the ground. The woman did as she learned in class and knocked the attacker off of her.

### *Kim, Florida*

Kim is a police officer for the state of Florida. She drove three hours to attend my seminar. Sadly, she could not participate due to an injury suffered on the job. Thus, the need for Krav Maga.

When she healed she returned to work. She was called to a home where domestic violence was reported. When she arrived, she found a large man in his "wife beater" T shirt, beating his wife.

Her Taser was not working and she did not want to pull out her hand gun. She called for backup. The aggressive man attacked her. Using a technique, she saw at the seminar she was able to knock him off balance. While he was stunned she handcuffed him.

When the backup arrived the wife beater was lying down peacefully, handcuffed.


Ms. E,

Mexico City

E is a young single mom, a widow. After only one Krav Maga seminar she found use for her newfound skills less than a month after the seminar.

As she was walking out of a hospital, feeling weak and sick, a man approached her and put a gun in her belly. She was terrified but had enough of crime and violence. She was tired of living in fear. So she did as she was taught at the seminar.

She not only caused the gun to fall from his hand and roll under a car, but he also broke some fingers and his wrist.


Kids of Maaleh Adumim.

Menachem was a skinny kid, bullied on a regular basis. He took up training with me. One day on the way home from school he had enough and fought back. He put the other kid in the hospital. Menachem's dad responded by pulling his son out of our program.

Bracha and Tehilla were being harassed by boys on their way home from school, teased and having their skirts pulled. The "tough guy" boys did not expect much resistance from two modest religious girls. They fought back; kicks and punches, and chased the boys away.

### *South Africa*

A young man, 18 years old, started training in South Africa. In his first six months of training twice he faced an armed gunman, and both times he successfully took the gun away.

Here is a report of an incident of one of our students in South Africa.

He was walking his dog when confronted by a larger hooligan type boy standing in front of Noorheuwel High School, this hooligan was out and out on the way to hurt Ian. Ian said more than once to the guy that he does not want to fight. The hooligan said to him he does care and he was going to "f**k him up.

Ian gave the dog to a young girl to hold and prepared for the fight. The young hooligan threw a semi hook-straight punch at Ian's face. Ian used the "IKI basic block" or my name for the technique the "Oh-shucks" to deflect the punch, Trapped the hooligans arm, and did an elbow strike on the idiot's face.

He then released the hooligan, pushed him off and again said that he did not want to fight.

The hooligan, with deflated ego, held his hand over his bleeding nose and went off having very little if any fight left in him.

The girl has now spread the word on Ian's ability and Ian has gained many friends and respect from the students at the school.

**D. Smith, South Africa**

I cannot remember all the stories, but there have been hundreds of them over the years and many more than never reached me. We are making a difference, taking a bite out of crime. We are not eliminating crime but it is a start.

Remember, when you are training, you are making an investment, an investment in yourselves and in your communities.

# Hysteria or Clear Thinking

AUGUST 27, 2015, ISRAEL

I was recently accused of being "hysterical". Rather insulting, to say the least, as not only do I see myself as the exact opposite of this (calm and clear thinking) but the term is usually ascribed to women (even the historical definition comes from women: *hysteria* referred to a medical condition thought to be particular to women and caused by disturbances of the uterus (from the Greek ὑστέρα hystera "uterus").

But let's look at the more modern use of the term: "Hysteria, in its colloquial use, describes unmanageable emotional excesses".

Why was I accused of this?

Are my concerns "excesses"?

Earlier this year my home was invaded, I was robbed and suffered terrible damage. Since then the criminals have returned at least three times. Thanks to my home protection and alert neighbors the criminals were unsuccessful.

From what I hear on the street our neighborhood is hit by home robberies about twice per month. For me this is reason for concern. We know who the criminals are, local Arabs, the police have confirmed this and have caught some of them For this reason the local rabbis have declared this situation one of "life and death" as a robbery can quickly turn into a murder.

On a community level I have tried to warn others. On a personal level I have taken measures to protect my home.

My initial measures proved only partially successful. Although the thieves did not get in they certainly showed determination. My defenses were not enough to deter them. They returned again with better tools and a better plan. So I invested even more in my home protection. And of course my Krav Maga training is there in case of a direct confrontation.

As a concerned citizen I want my neighbors to be aware of the situation. I do not want anyone to experience what I, and so many others, have recently experienced. I want a public campaign to raise awareness like they do with driving in America. They have those signs...."134 people killed on this highway", or outside US military basis "23 days with no drunk driving related deaths".

This gets your attention and makes you think. Everyone slows down.

For suggesting this idea a woman referred to me again and again as "hysterical" and causing "panic". Such people are like those Jews who knew what was coming during the Holocaust but "kept things quiet" so as to avoid spreading "hysterics". We all know the results of such clever policies.

Yes, I want people to be scared, to wake up! to take action. That is exactly what I do with Krav Maga. Do not wait until it is your little girl who was raped and murdered and cut up into little pieces. Take action now.

I want people to stop fooling themselves and wake up to reality, before it is too late.

You cannot shut me down with insults.

*"I have always thought it was a most valuable trait to recognize reality and not to pursue delusions. But when I now think over my life up to and including the years of imprisonment, there was no period in which I was free of delusory notions."* (Inside the Third Reich, Albert Speer, page 291)

Albert Speer wrote those words while serving a twenty-year sentence for his participation in the Third Reich of Germany. He describes how easy it was to fool himself, and how everyone reinforced everyone else.

We are all humans, Jews, Germans, all of us. The Jews fooled themselves into believing that "it could not happen", the Germans fooled themselves into believing "It is not actually happening". But...we all go along with what we are supposed to believe. After all, no one wants to be accused of being "Hysterical"!!

# Krav Maga Gentle Warriors

August 28, 2015, Israel

We have a vision.

Krav Maga is about self-defense, but self-defense is not only physical, far from it.

I would say the vast majority of defensive work in Israel is not physical. Female IDF soldiers monitoring the borders with electronic devices, all sorts of "smart technology" that I cannot even begin to understand. And attitude.

I recall something Prime Minister Gold Meir said when I was just a child, "We can forgive the Arabs for killing our children, but we cannot forgive them for turning our children into killers."

Let's think about that.

Yes, in war, and we are at war, there is a need for brutality at times. But the question is...will this change who we are?

Let's be honest, we have come a long way from the downtrodden Jew of the European *shtetl* (village) to the IDF warrior of today. The question is how much has really changed?

As I point out in my book, *Israel, A Nation of Warriors,* a portion of our people have always retained their fighting spirit, even in the darkest of times, we remained fighters.

Today of course we are in a far better position. The key is, can we return to the Hebrew warrior of old?

Today many of our people lament the "New Jew". Yes, he may be tough, perhaps too tough. Perhaps some of our modern warriors are not modeling themselves after our own ancient Hebrew warriors but after warrior concepts that are foreign to our nation. Perhaps they see themselves as "superior elite beings" (like the Nazis), a new breed of men or women.

Prancing about the ring showing off your muscles after a sporting event victory is not our concept of a true warrior. The true warrior does not behave this way; they do what must be done and go about it quietly.

*Moshe with a couple of true warriors.*

A true warrior does not boast about his military career.

My fear is that some of the "New Jew" warriors have lost their "Jewishness" they have lost the sweetness and sensitivity. The Torah proclaims young David as a great warrior, *"Saul has slain his thousands, and David his tens of thousands."* (1 Samuel 18:7) but David is also referred to as "The Sweet Singer of Israel".

Moses was a great leader, and the "humblest of all men". Deborah was a woman who tried to stay out of the spotlight, but when she was needed she led her people in battle.

Abraham was a man of God, a man of peace but also a warrior. He never showed off his fighting skills until it was absolutely necessary.

Our vision, the IKI way, is the way of the ancient Hebrew warrior, a gentle warrior, a man of peace who knows how to fight when he has too. We are not seeking bullies, we are not looking for bravado.

Our instructors will never challenge another instructor or a student to a fight of any sort.

Our instructors will never endanger a student or colleague by training with live weapons of any type.

Our instructors will never "shoot off at the mouth". These are the requirements for IKI instructors. Be honest, be truthful, be loyal. This is our model and these are our goals.

Abraham was not "soft".

Moses was not "soft".

Ehud ben Gerah, David, Saul, Samuel....none of them were "soft", but all were gentle warriors.

Isaac says to his son Jacob... *"The voice is the voice of Jacob but the hands are the hands of Esau"* (Genesis 27:22)

Rabbi Y. Kahane writes, *"The gentleness of manner and the voice is that of Jacob, but the hands are those of Esau."* In other words, we can fight!

We see this as a message for all future generations of warriors; be gentle in your manners, in your speech, as was our father Jacob, but when you need to fight be as tough as Esau.

# Employee or Leader
### August 29, 2015

A president or a prime minister is the leader of a nation but he is also an employee. His salary is being paid by all the citizens of the land and, at least in theory, he must answer to we the people or else we the people can fire him.

Is one a leader or an employee, or something in between?

In the old days there were kings were ruled by "divine right", they truly believed that God had chosen them and their family line to rule forever. Those days are pretty much over with. We choose our leaders and they work for us, but they also must guide us.

So when we look at our political leaders, our spiritual and religious leaders, and our martial arts leaders, we must ask; employee or leader, or both?

Let's take a look at rabbis. In the "Old Country" (Europe before the war) there was no question. The rabbi was the leader. If a rabbi was already well known the congregation would simply send him a request asking if he would be willing to assume leadership of their community. If he was lesser known the rabbi might be invited for a Sabbath. He would speak to the people, deliver a sermon, conduct services and teach classes, and then the community would make a decision.

Once the decision was made and the new rabbi was chosen, that was it! Now he became the undisputed leader. His word was the word of God and it would be followed by all.

Yes, his salary was being paid by the community, every man must eat, but he was never regarded as an "employee".

In Israel this is still the model. In large communities, the rabbi's salary is paid by the municipality and in smaller communities it is often a volunteer job. The rabbi makes his living by teaching. But outside of Israel, in the more modern atmosphere, this has changed. In many places it is made clear to the rabbi that he must follow, not lead.

My father had a colleague years ago who lost his job. He was fired. This rabbi had served his congregation faithfully for many years but times were changing. This was in California. The rabbi was told to adapt the religion to the changing desires of the members. The rabbi refused to comply.

When the rabbi was fired a letter was sent out to the members explaining this decision. The words were shocking. *"The rabbi was fired because he refused to see himself as an employee of the synagogue. He imagined himself to be the leader."*

Imagine that?

Whoa to the congregation that refuses to be led.

### *Martial Arts*

In the traditional arts there was the do, the way. The teacher, the sensei, was seen as the guide, the leader. But now is the sensei your employee? Are you his student or his client? Is he just being hired to do a job?

Do you treat your teacher as an employee or as a revered master? Does he need to answer to you, or you to him? Should you treat e mails from him as important, or ...I will get to it when I can?

I always have, and still do, treat my teachers as parental figures, with the utmost respect. My students know that when Itay would call me I take the call, during class or at any time. And if he needed me to teach a class my students knew that I would go and one of my students would fill in for me at our school. That is how you treat a teacher, with Respect.

When I speak to my teacher on the phone, I stand! Respect.

Ultimately it is your choice; student or client, teacher or employee, rabbi or some guy whom we pay to work at the synagogue.

Your choice will be a reflection of you who are, and in what circles you will be welcomed.

All great rabbis were the disciples of great teachers. This is how our tradition continues to be passed on for more than 3,000 years, unbroken despite endless persecution.

Don't break the chain.

Moses received the Torah from Mt. Sinai and gave it over to Joshua. Joshua gave it over to the Elders, the Elders to the Prophets, and the Prophets gave it over to the Men of the Great Assembly.

... and so it continues to our very day....

# Getting Good at It
SEPTEMBER 1, 2015, BUSINESS LOUNGE, BEN GURION AIRPORT

I felt kind of proud of myself today. As I put my suitcase on the scale at the airport it registered 23 kilos. Exactly Twenty-Three kilo, which is the amount allowed for each suitcase.

I felt proud, in a funny sort of way, because I judged it on my own, without a scale. I got it right, just by the feel of it.

I travel a lot teaching Krav Maga seminars around the world. Airports are my second home. With time I am getting good at this. I know what to do and where to go. In each airport I can find the Starbucks, the El Al terminal, the men's room and the right business lounge.

If we do something long enough...we get good at it. If we neglect it long enough we lose our skill, our touch.

I sometimes wonder...I know guys who are pilots and they do Krav Maga. I know guys who are all sorts of things and they do Krav Maga. But I just do Krav Maga. I teach, I train, I watch, I analyze. And if you do something long enough you get good at it. You just can't help it. Talk to a guy who has been laying bricks for decades and you will be amazed at how much he knows. And you thought there was not much to it.

Sometimes I wonder; that guy can fly a plane and does Krav Maga, but I can't fly the plane! But the difference is that my eyes are both on Krav Maga. So I pick up things that others do not. This is not the only thing that I do of course but it is my only "job". It is what I focus on every day, day in and day out.

So I see more Krav students than most local teachers can imagine. I pick up the subtleties that the part time guys miss. I pick up things that others miss.

When you do something long enough you get pretty good at it. You notice the little things that others miss, and that makes all the difference.

# Be the Storm
### September 7, 2015, Norway

I do not like to hurt people. Do not confuse this with being weak, or soft.

I do not like to hurt my students, or others, during training; it is not necessary and contributes nothing to self-defense ability.

If possible I always strive to avoid a fight. Do not confuse this with being afraid of a fight. For when I need to be in a fight I become the storm. And when a storm comes it is best to stay home, where you are safe.

Too many people feel a need to prove themselves by hurting others, or even by hurting themselves. They want the injuries to prove their supposed toughness. They wear an injury as a badge of honor.

Injuries may and do happen, but we do not seek them to prove anything. We train to avoid harm, not to invite it.

I always stress to my students, and to seminar participants; do not confuse what you see on the outside as a sign of weakness. Be careful not to draw conclusions when you do not understand the person you see.

The outside is a cultivated kindness, a softness that reflects a calm spirit, a spirit that is the result of an inner spiritual quest. But alongside this calmness is an iron wall and an iron will. There is a stubborn power inside that will not be denied. There is a 3,700 year man with a lot of "issues". Do not push.

There is a powder keg that can be ignited at a moments' notice. Press the wrong button and you may be in serious trouble. Yes, there is total self-control but that control is not limited to "softness", that control switch can be switched to the On button and a storm can be unleashed.

I will never allow someone else to control these buttons. I will not fight because someone else is in the more for a fight, or a so called "Challenge".

If you challenge me to a fight, and I accept, it means that you have already won, for your will power overtook mine.

No, I will not accept your challenge. I will not fight simply because you are in the mood for a fight. No, never. I will never allow you to choose the time and the place of a fight. I reserve that right for myself. I am in control, not you.

Being in control means you do not allow anyone to draw you into a fight against your will. If you must fight you will chose the time and place. And if you are attacked and you have no choice but to defend yourself...you will become the storm and unleash a force that will make your assailant regret he ever tried.

Be calm and keep the storm inside...until you decide it is time to unleash it.

In a letter written in 1900, a year before he became president, Theodore Roosevelt wrote, *"I have always been fond of the West African proverb: `Speak softly and carry a big stick; you will go far.'"*

## COMMENTS

Moshe sir, I love this blog. The storm we see and hear, we can prepare for. It is the quiet storm which represents the most immediate threat and destruction. I've had instructors who believe they need to hurt their students to prove their arts worthiness. I have seen martial artists who feel the need to intimidate others or fight on a whim to prove their bravado. Nope, I am with you. I choose when, where, and I will be the quiet storm. There is no honor in being a bully. There is only righteousness in acting in true defense of yourself or others. Psalm 82:4 Have a great day!

*Dan McGee*

# One Man's Perspective
SEPTEMBER 7, 2015 OSLO, NORWAY

*No one I think is in my tree*

*I mean it must be high or low (Lennon and McCartney, but really ...Lennon)*

John Lennon, what a man. When I began to glimpse the meaning behind his lyrics I began to see the genius that John Lennon was.

When you are different you begin to feel either I am smarter than everyone else or something is wrong with me. Either way no one is in my tree. I am alone over here. So I must be high or low but I am certainly not the same as everyone else.

Why am I asking questions that no one else is asking?

Why am I coming up with solutions that no one else is thinking of?

I must be high or low.

The questions can lead us far from our starting point. It can lead us to uncomfortable zones. It can lead us to our own tree, or perhaps others begin to see things as we do and join us.

Does not matter, we ask the questions and we face the consequences.

Some call it a slippery slope but I say if we do not ask these questions we become fossils and we are only relevant to palaeontologists and historians.

We want to be relevant.

At IKI we ask questions, we accept all questions…

This morning in Frogner, once again we tackled a few new situations.

I took our top instructor, Morten Wang and one his best students, Instructor Trond Stenberg.

We took a very bad situation and tested our method and the methods of competing approaches and we tried it until we were satisfied.

I always say, be fair. Do not favor my approach over that of anyone else. If they have found a better solution, we shall adopt it, but that did not happen. We openly question everything and we honestly seek solutions. If it does not work for our students and instructors we must drop it and find a better solution.

Honesty and integrity above all.

# Who Are You?

### September 8, 2015, Israel

*Well, who are you?*
*I really wanna know*
*Tell me, who are you?*
*'Cause I really wanna know (Pete Townshend?)*

We want to know who you are.

Why?

Because we want to know if you are worth our time, if you are genuine, if you are worth listening to, if your qualifications are up to standard. That is why the back flap of the book always tells a little about the author. That is why all books of Jewish learning seek approval of the most learned men.

We want to know who you are before we become your students. We do not want to buy your fake magic potions. A fool and his money are quickly parted.

Do not be a fool.

*Training with Prof. Cohen, a lighter moment but always deadly serious.*

In my early seminar days I had the great privilege of having one of my mentors observe me in action. He critiqued me. He helped me grow.

He watched me. He took notes, kept writing. What was he writing? What was I doing wrong?

After the seminar he came over and we went over his notes, point by point. His words of wisdom have greatly impacted me, his personal example, his integrity and honestly set an example for me.

It is wonderful to have a teacher.

His first remark caught me a little by surprise. Who are you? You did not introduce yourself, why?

I explained that I did not want to waste the participants' valuable time talking about myself and my credentials, my history and accomplishments.

But I was wrong

Who are you? We really want to know.

Prof. Cohen explained that he always introduces himself at the beginning of a seminar, and trust me, you will not meet a more humble man. The man not only embodies a true gentleman but everything you would ever hope to find in a true martial artist.

He does not look the part, he is not short and Asian, he is tall and Jewish, but he is the martial artist you have been hoping to meet. But do not call him "Master" he does not like that. To him that brings back the image of master and slave, just call him Mr. Cohen.

So Prof. Cohen, a.k.a. Mr. Cohen, says we should start a seminar with introducing ourselves, assuming we are not known to the students. Sadly, I have been lacking in this area and I really must take a few minutes at a seminar to tell you a little about myself.

But why?

Who are you? We really want to know. And you really should know.

Who is your electrician? Is he a licensed union man? Did he serve as an apprentice under a master craftsman? Who is he?

Do you really want him playing around with your electricity when you do not know who he is?

You need to know who he is, you need to know if he is trained and certified or "self taught". That is why we have union certification. For a man to fix your phone he needs to have the proper training and certification. Should your life be any less important?

Who are you? We really want to know.

We want to know if you are an honest man whom we can trust. We want to know you are using union grade materials. We want to know you are not making it up as you go along.

Why should Krav Maga be any different?

Recently Rob Wallace from Georgia, USA, wrote me that in all the many times we have trained together I have never hurt him. You want that on your resume. If you are bringing your child into a class you want to know that the instructor is responsible, that he will not hurt anyone.

You want to know that the instructor is not going to use live weapons, ever!

You want to know that your instructor trained for many years under the watchful eye of other respected instructors.

You know my teachers, you can contact them, ask them about me. You can ask for my certifications from all over the world. My certifications are publicly available. I have lived and taught in the same community for more than twenty years, just come here and ask anyone. I have raised a generation; they have all served in the Israel Defense Forces with honor.

I am very proud of my work.

That is what you want from an instructor, you want to know who they are.

*Who are you? Yes, we really want to know.*

We want to know that you are not making up your own military records. We want to know that you are not making up your own certifications.

We want to know whom you trained and who trained you.

# Grandfather~Godfather

### SEPTEMBER 9, 2015, ISRAEL

We need parents and we need grandparents. We need roots and we need someone to look up to. We need role models and we need someone to talk with, someone with life experience and wisdom. We need guidance.

Joseph said that the image of his father Jacob was always with him. When he was sold into Egyptian slavery, far from home and facing many difficult challenges the image of his father Jacob guided him.

> We are told...may your eyes always behold the image of your teachers. (Isaiah chapter 30, verse 20)

וְהָיוּ עֵינֶיךָ רֹאוֹת אֶת מוֹרֶיךָ

We need our grandfathers.

But grandfathers do not last forever. They are a limited gift. My grandfather Moe passed away before I was born. My grandfather Isaac was a great rabbi and a true role model. But he too was gone during my 17th year.

We seek grandfathers; guides, teachers, role models, advisers...throughout our lives.

During our lives we gather information, experiences, tidbits of wisdom. Hopefully we read, we study, we spend time with the wise ones. As the rabbis wrote 2,000 years ago, "hanging out" with your teachers is the same as studying from them, the "simple chatter" of the teachers is regarded as wisdom and is an important part of our education and growth. If you find a true teacher...stick with him.

But not all men grow up to be grandfathers. Some just grow big, some grow fat, some just grow old. Some grow greedy, grumpy and angry.

Words of wisdom are always all around us, the question is do we listen, do we hear, do we embrace.

We need the Godfather, a wise old man to settle disputes, resolve differences and guide diverse people to a common goal. We need a godfather that all parties respect to make a fair decision.

And then comes a time when some of us, reluctantly perhaps, must embrace the role of grandfather/godfather. We must become the grandfather. We must rise above greed, above jealousy, above anger. We must control the situation rather than be controlled by it. We must remain balanced.

Years ago when I consulted with a rabbi in Brooklyn about Krav Maga he said to me...there is no one for you to follow, you must become the Zaide (grandfather in Yiddish).

I still turn to my teachers for advice, and guidance, but as the rabbi said I must be the Zaide, the grandfather.

The words of my father, and my grandfathers, are always with me. The soft spoken ways of grandfather Isaac, the revolutionary Zionist fire and passion of grandfather Moe, the dream, the ideal.

Not all are fit to lead. Just yesterday on the plane while chatting with a fellow Israeli she said to me, *"What a heavy name you carry, Moshe David from the family of priests, these are names of leadership."*

We believe names mean a great deal. Moshe and David were great Jewish leaders. My parents gave me a lot to live up to.

I hope I am worthy of this holy task.

# Hands Up Baby

September 10, 2015, Israel

I heard a song called "Hands Up Baby", I hate it. But apparently this is what a lot of instructors base their Krav Maga on.

When I teach Krav Maga around the world and I approach the topic of handgun defense I see that students (and instructors from other styles of Krav Maga) automatically pick up their hands. Like the silly song, *Hands up Baby*. They seem to do this without thinking, an automatic response. There is a gun; first thing we do is pick up our hands.

But why?

Is no one but me thinking?

There are certain cases where we do take that extra step of raising our hands, however...that is *only* in certain cases where we must do so in order to bring our hands to a better position. We bring our hands closer to our intended target and we improve our leverage. (i.e. our strength and ability to take the gun away, not relying upon speed or muscle but on body position and leverage).

So we have accomplished two things: We are closer to our intended target, and we have better leverage.

However in most gun defense situations this is not the case. Yet everyone else in the Krav Maga world seems to be automatically picking up their hands.

Why is this a problem?

This is a major problem, a major error that could cost you your life.

*They are making two major mistakes*

1. They are wasting valuable time. All this "please don't shoot me Sir" is taking up precious time. You are engaging with the enemy for too long. There is no guarantee that while you are grovelling and begging the assailant is waiting for you. Never assume he is falling for your acting routine. Criminals are not fools.

*Every second counts!*

Do not waste valuable time. Do not waste a step raising your hands unless there is no other option. Instructors who teach the hands up approach are putting you at a much greater risk.

2. In most cases this "hands up" approach will actually put you in a position with very poor leverage. While watching videos, it may look good, it may appear as if the defender is easily taking the gun away, but remember - that is acting! Those are his students and this is a choreographed video. It is no more real than the cool antics you see on TV. Do not be fooled by a video. Life is not a movie.

I stress not to automatically go to the hands up approach but to understand distance, timing, psychology, body position and leverage. All this is part of our approach. We are a thinking system. Not all Krav Maga is the same.

An educated person is our best student. The head is not built for head butts, it is built for thinking.

# Got Skills
## September 11, 2015

Nature vs. Nurture, Attitude or Skill? Which is more important and which plays a greater role in our lives.

This brings up the question of Attitude and Technique/Skill in martial arts and self-defense.

Is having a tough attitude enough?

Certainly it helps, and certainly it is important. But clearly it is not enough.

When approached with danger, threats, it is certainly important not to show fear, not to grovel, cry or beg, (even if it is only fake, still wrong and dangerous). It is important to play the Rocky, Clint Eastwood type, show some attitude, be strong and confident. In many cases this will be enough to cause the enemy to back off.

But of course before then we should try the soft approach, i.e. appease the person with some kind words, *soft words turn back anger*. Only when the soft words of appeasement fail should we turn up the tough guy attitude.

Soft words spoken with confidence, being kind but coming from a position of strength is, I believe, the best approach.

Now what about if all this fails and things turn violent. Is attitude enough?

We all know of some cases where an enraged woman, seeking to defend her small children, rampaged into a bigger and stronger man and simply overpowered him with her attitude and anger. But...we also know that in most cases this ends in disaster.

Even in the recent case where some American Marines on vacation in Paris tackled and disarmed a terrorist, they got shot. Clearly they lacked self-defense training and skill. Many people die trying to defend others.

*Attitude is not enough.*

In any aspect of life attitude will only get you so far. You need skills, real skills and the only way to get skills is to train.

You must train.

You want to be a licensed plumber? Take a course. You want to be a teacher; you must study in a quality university. Attitude will only go so far. Where attitude runs out skills take over. You need skills.

Some people go through life complaining bitterly about their lousy fate, why do others get all the breaks?

Why? Because others worked hard. Because others studied.

There is no shortcut in life. You must train, you must study.

You want to be a great guitar player, you will have to spend many hours each day playing, but not just playing, studying scales, doing special drills. It ain't all fun n' games.

Running at a terrorist who is armed with an AK 47, well, it is brave and praiseworthy but wouldn't it be better if you had actually trained in Krav Maga and learned how to disarm an attacker *without* getting shot?

Success: it comes to those who work hard, train hard, fight hard to get what they want. Attitude is a good start but it sure is not enough.

We have all seen those video clips were cute girls in tiny little shorts take down guys and put them in a sleeper choke or something, embarrassing but those girls have skills. The boys had only attitude.

Krav Maga is here to give you not only a fighting spirit and great attitude but the skills to go along with it. Attitude without skills is like a check book on an empty bank account. There is nothing to back up the check. Attitude will not cut it.

Now stop whining about your poor lot in life and start training.

# Class Act

September 15, 2015, Israel, a new year begins...

*"Eagles don't hunt flies." (Mob quotes)*

I often quote lessons learned from gangsters. I am a student of the classic American gangster era, not to glorify, dignify or justify in any way but, there are lessons to be learned.

We can learn from any source.

1. **Never Grovel** - Read the gangster books, see the documentaries, even in the face of death the classic Jewish and Italian mobsters never grovelled or begged. Perhaps some of the lower "foot soldiers" did, but never the leaders. Even in the face of death, show dignity, do not lose your cool or composure, do not resort to baseless insults. Class. Always, but always, speak from a position of strength.

Some of the more famous gangsters actually asked for the option of taking their own lives, to die an honorable death. If a death sentence was pronounced, it was accepted, solemnly.

2. **Honor** - Yes, honor. There was honor and respect among the gangsters. A word was a word. Deals were made with handshakes, nothing more.

3. **Loyalty** - These organizations were ruthless but the members were loyal to each other. You were loyal to your godfather. If he needed a favor from you, you did it. You showed your gratitude for all he did for you.

4. **Honesty** - The mob was built on trust and honesty, not on contracts or legal documents of course. If you promised to pay a man, you paid him. Lack of honesty was severally punished. Business depended on honesty.

> *A deal was a deal and it was honored. A man who would not honor his deal, would not do business any more.*

5. **Generosity** - Loyalty and hard work was rewarded with extra pay. Mayer Lansky stressed to always tip and tip big at restaurants. This is simply good business. When the police come the waitress will alert you and get you to safety. Being generous is good for business, any business.

6. **Motivation** - Lansky stressed that they were always looking for good young men. They wanted men with true ambition. A hard working loyal young man with ambition could go very far, very fast.

7. **Courage** - You need courage to act. And you need courage to face the consequences of your actions. If you made a mistake, you paid for it.

8. **Don't talk too much** - Did Mayer Lansky retire with 300 million dollars or a few thousand? 'till today no one knows. Was he the master of all American crime or simply an accountant? We still do not know. Keep your mouth shut unless you have something important to say.

**Stay out of needless arguments.**

Do not engage a fool in rhetoric. Serious people have more important things to do than argue with fools of no significance. Never honor a fool with an argument. Do not allow him to steal your precious time.

9. **Pay your bills on time** - Never give anyone an opportunity to bring charges against you. Pay and pay on time. Do not delay payment, bad for business. Leave no doubt that all debts are fully paid up.

10. **Don't brag** - No one likes a big mouth. If you truly are great, people will know it. A lot of hot air usually means there is very little content. Big talkers can never compete with big doers.

And finally, in summation, **Dignity** - Always carry yourself with dignity. Did you ever see those mobsters walking around looking like thugs or bums? Were they dressed like homeless people? No, they were always dressed in expensive suits. They saw themselves as businessmen. Yes, they did kill at times, but so do governments. (Of course I am not justifying this, only explaining their point of view.)

They displayed class, self-control, dignity. Certainly we, martial artists, instructors and students alike, should behave accordingly. Avoid arguments but welcome discussion, avoid insults but welcome constructive ideas, show respect at all times.

And remember, no one ever disrespected the godfather.

## Mob Quotes

*Do Not Lie*

*"I never lie to any man because I don't fear anyone. The only time you lie is when you are afraid" ~ John Gotti*

*"Our principles are highest; honor, solidarity and vengeance. We know there's no justice for us except we earn it. We earn respect."*

*Team Work*

*"It takes many steppingstones, you know, for a man to rise. None can do it unaided" ~ Joe Bonanno*

*Do Not Attempt a Knife Disarm*

*"Run from a knife and rush a gun." ~ Jimmy Hoffa*

*"The best armor is to keep out of range."*

*Strong Will*

*"If there is a will, there is always a way my friend" ~ Richard Kuklinski*

*"Men stumble on stones, not mountains."*

## Maintain your Dignity

*"Eagles don't hunt flies."*

## Watch Your Mouth

*"Don't let your tongue be your worst enemy."*
~ John Franseze

*"Never open your mouth, unless you're in the dentist chair"* ~ *Sammy* "The Bull" Gravano

## Be Realistic

*"Every remedy of a bad situation has its bad side effects. Choose the remedy with the least."*

## Miscellaneous

*"I have killed no men, that, in the first place, didn't deserve killing"* ~ *Mickey Cohen*

*Taxes*

"Always overpay your taxes. That way you'll get a refund." ~ Meyer Lansky

*Honesty*

"I am an American citizen, first class. I don't have a badge that makes me an official good guy like you, but I work just as honest for a living. ~ Lucky Luciano

"Accept that certain things are beyond your control. Let it be".

"I have no control over anybody" ~ Tony Accardo

*Maintain Your Principles and Expect Trouble*

"A man without enemies is a man without qualities. Even Jesus Christ had many enemies."

"The world belongs to the patient man."

"When you compromise, you lose. When you seem to have compromise, you have taken a step towards winning."

*Live with Courage*

*"It's better to live on day as a lion than a hundred years as a lamb"* ~ John Gotti

*"There isn't anything on earth that I will hide from or back up from"* ~ Greg Scarpa

*Kindness or Weakness*

*"Don't mistake my kindness for weakness. I am kind to everyone, but when someone is unkind to me, weak is not what you are going to remember about me"* ~ Al Capone

## Non-Mob Quotes

*"When the debate is lost, slander becomes the tool of the loser."* **Socrates**

*"My dear friends never enter into a war of words as the battle is lost"*, **Tony Preston**

*"Name calling is the last refuge of the non-thinkers"*, **Rabbi Meir Kahane**

# Guarantees

*September 16, 2015, Israel*

*In this world nothing can be said to be certain, except death and taxes. (Benjamin Franklin)*

We all want guarantees in life. We want to know that our parents will always love us. We want to know that our friends will never betray us. We want to know that our colleagues will not stab us in the back.

We want many things.

We want to know that our home is safe from invasion. We want to know that we will pass the course. We want to know that our marriage will work, that our loved ones will never leave us.

We want to know that our friends will not die on us too soon.

But none of this is true. And there are no guarantees of any sort, only that someday you will die and you will have to pay some taxes. Death is certain…life is a question mark.

So do not expect guarantees in Krav Maga either. But we will do our very best to help. We will train hard, we will spare no expense, we will investigate every situation you ask about, and those that you never thought of. We will try everything full force and full resistance, but then we guarantee nothing.

I can only guarantee that we will do our best.

My teacher never claimed to be a humble man. In fact that was not even a virtue he was striving for, just the opposite. But he was always honest, deadly serious and honest.

He fought hard with us, we paid our dues. For eighteen years I fought full-contact three times each week; Kickboxing, Muay Thai, BJJ and MMA. I have seen the insides of more than one hospital. We train honest.

But there are no guarantees, in life, or in self-defense. A random made up technique...might work. An experienced black belt...might fail. But, what he always stressed was...improve your chances. *"Chance favors the prepared"* ***(Louis Pasteur)***

What Louis Pasteur meant, put in a Krav Maga perspective, is that while life is unpredictable, a prepared person will seize opportunities; he will see opportunities where others do not. That is why you must train in Krav Maga. Being tough is not enough. Skill matters. When everything goes to hell your training will matter, so train correctly.

We have no guarantees, even the best techniques, someone might see it coming, someone might be nervous and turn the other way. Human reactions can be sudden and unpredictable. That is why it is so easy, and so unfair, to mock the techniques of another style.

We can all make our techniques look great, and we can all take someone else's techniques and make them look ridiculous. But that is simply not fair. Our goal is never to mock any technique or style, only to find what works best for the average person.

We try our very best to be honest. We tear every technique apart, our own and those of others. We stick with what we believe to be the best but if we found something out there that was better, we would use it!

Your life matters much more than our desire to say "see, I was right". All that matters is that we give you the best chance of getting home safe.

# Realistic Expectations

SEPTEMBER 17, 2015, ISRAEL

*You can't always get what you want.... but if you try sometimes you just might find, you get what you need.*

Yes, like many of you I grew up with that song, when the Rolling Stones, and us, were young. You live, you learn. You can't always get what you want but in the end we all make it happen. Only it does not always happen the way we thought it would.

For example I became a Krav Maga instructor despite the fact that when I was younger I was sure that my destiny was to be the Jewish Jimi Hendrix. At 17 I knew I was going to be like the guitar heroes of my age, Clapton, Hendrix, Jimmy Page, George Harrison, Santana, Tony Iommi, Jeff Beck, Keith Richards...

But we do not always get what we want and we need to learn that, fast.

Life lessons...some of us want to be basketball stars but ...we lack the height, we do what we can. Some of want to be brain surgeons but we have no head for details. Some of us want to be a concert pianist but we have short stubby fingers.

**You can't always get what you want....**

No you can't always get what you want...but if you try sometimes you just might find you get what you need.

### *Krav Maga...*

At IKI we will only teach you what you can use. You might want to defend yourself with a cool back-spinning jump kick, you might want to grab the guy and flip him over your head, you might want to look like the cool Kung Fu guys in the movies but those are not realistic expectations. Perhaps there are super athletes who can do that, but it is not me or you. It is not your average person who can only devote three hours per week to training.

I do not care about what "works" on video, I care what works for you, when you are tired, fatigued, not in the mood.

We want to prevent your world from turning black..."*I could not foresee this thing happening to you*" **(Rolling Stones)**

We train with realistic expectations. We may not always give you what you want but we will give you what you need. And that my friends is the reality of life.

Some of you may know that I am not a great singer...can't really change that. We do what we can and we get by.

**Here we go....** You can't always get what you want.

But if you try...

So we try and we give you realistic tools. We create realistic expectations. We will stick to what you can do under stress. We will stick to what you can do after an injury, we will stick to what you can do when you are no longer young and fit.

We all grow old, or at least the wise and lucky ones among us.

# Clouds
### September 18, 2015, Israel

*When will those clouds all disappear? (Angie, Rolling Stones)*

We are born, we face challenges, some kids end up on the street. Some kids never make it to adulthood. Some kids grow old before their time.

No one said it would be easy.

Some are born into wonderful families, love and care and all that money can buy. Even some of those end up on the street.

And then...many people just get lost...lost in life, lost in themselves. Some fight to survive, some give up. And some find a helping hand, someone who cares enough to look at them.

We have to try. Life has so much to offer but yet so much potential for pain, loneliness.

*"Remember all those nights we cried"*

*All those dreams we held so close all seemed to go up in smoke*

Where are your dreams? Where are your goals? Where are your values?

*"Where will it lead us from here?"*

Where do we turn? Where do we turn to pick up the pieces? I feel that Krav Maga is one solution, one way to pick yourself up, grab a hold of your life and shout out loud I WANT TO LIVE

*Aint' it good to be alive...*

We have to remember that. We have to try and help others.

*I hate that sadness in your eyes...*

Are there clouds in your eyes? Is there something preventing you from seeing the truth clearly?

Think about your decisions, what are they based on? Clear rational thinking or fear, shame, pain, anger, wasted emotion?

Get up in the morning with a feeling of Awe. Say Damn it's good to be alive and face the new day. Find something that motivates you, something that *"wild horses could not drag you away"* from.

I have two friends...one is in a hospice, he can no longer speak, another is going through treatment for lung cancer. I have known both for a long time, one for over 30 years, the other since 1969.

Say it out loud I WANT TO LIVE and mean it. Wild horses couldn't drag me away...

Our Krav Maga is here to help people. Train not only to defeat your opponents but also to defeat the demons inside of you. Be a better person. Stand up for something. Bring joy to the world not darkness. Speak the truth.

I love the letters from our students where they write me that IKI Krav Maga has given them a new lease on life, a life worth living. Beyond the life saving skills that we give our students I know we are also giving them a "spiritual" base. Regardless of your faith, religion, or whatever, these values are universal; Life lessons.

*"So let's do some living"* **(Rolling Stones)**

*"Wild wild horses, we will ride them someday...."*

We want to help you open your eyes, and wash those clouds away. Learn to ride those wild horses.

Clear your thinking from foggy clouds, see clearly now....you can't always get what you want but first you need to know what you want, and clear those clouds away and see clearly.

So stop, clear your glasses, clear those clouds from your vision. Live honestly, train honestly. Treat people with kindness, even more kindness than they deserve. You will be happier for it.

# Krav Leadership Challenges

SEPTEMBER 19, 2015

Leadership is not easy and most people are not cut out for it. Whether you are the leader of a small group or a large nation, you will face serious challenges.

People will challenge your authority, your leadership ability, your goals and direction. After a while someone else might feel that you have lost your edge and they are more suited to replace you. The king is dead, long live the king.

It ain't easy.

I want all of you to know something; you are not alone. As I said, whether you are an instructor with a few students, or head of an international organization this will happen. Someone will think they know better than you, someone will get insulted over nothing, you will soon find yourself feeling more like a babysitter for adults than a martial arts instructor.

There are days I dream of being a street cleaner. Honest.

On my mother's side I have traced my family line back to the Jewish leaders of Babylon. They held the position of *Resh Galutha,* Head of the Exiled People, or Exilarch.

The first one to hold this position in our family was Shealtiel from the year 586 BCE. The position was held in the family for centuries.

This is what is written in history about the position.

*"Moreover, in order for the position to work it required an almost superhuman individual. An ordinary person would be broken by the job because of the **conflicting demands and pressures**. The Jewish people were fortunate enough that at least half the time – perhaps 70% of the time – they had such super-people. Under their leadership, the Jewish community prospered and was able to keep at bay the pagan authorities at the same time controlling **internal divisions** within the community."*

Now remember these words were written about a job held by my family and others from over 2,500 years ago!

Has anything changed? No. People are not easy. Moses himself complained bitterly about his position of leadership. So I hope this brings some comfort to all of you out there. Hang in there.

Recently one of our long term IKI members wrote me a heartfelt letter about some problems he was facing. I am deleting the details and names in order not to embarrass anyone. Our purpose is to learn, not to embarrass.

*"Moshe,*

*I had a very similar situation where I was basically threatened to give rank or they will go elsewhere. The guy had made yellow belt barely-he always complained that we were doing the same thing etc-but when we did anything else he would get hurt I call them phantom injuries. This was the only time in my entire martial arts experience that I had a guy train a few months and think he knew more than everyone- He had money, lots of it and was a great client until I didn't sell him any rank- He was OK as long as we had a cooperating partner but when he had to spar even if it was light contact if he got hit he would sit in the floor and cry-His wife would then berate me and they would threaten to leave and they tried to shut me down by talking to the rest of the class about me in a negative way-*

*Long story short they no longer train with me- I survived their cowardly attacks-the only thing I regret is that he even got his yellow belt.*

*It was a lesson learned for me even with all my many years of experience this was a first. My goal isn't to hurt anyone but to pass along survival skills- when a student of such low rank sets out to cause you problems and question decisions you have made in your personal life and slander you but then smile in your face during class it's an eye opener. I'm sure in your position it happens a lot.*

*My reply was if they questioned my decisions so much maybe they should look at the certificate and belt I had signed for them and ask themselves-if they really deserved it and are they honoring the system by being a backstabber.*

*I am a lifelong IKI Krav Maga Practitioner I love to train under pressure and in diverse conditions, I thrive in scenario training. The IKI has helped mould me into a better person, I thank you for allowing me to be a part of it-it's a family. In my town I am mainly a personal trainer and run fitness programs but when we do our self defense we take it serious- Thank you for all you do."*

(editor's note; now that he passed away let me see it was our dear friend Gary Hodges who wrote this)

I wanted to share this letter with all of you because I know we all have this sort of experience from time to time, on one level or another.

People will criticize us, but remember, this is not a reflection on us or the work that we do. Look at who is saying it and take it in the proper proportion. I myself have been told by an 18-year-old Dutch fellow that I do not know how to teach very well. Guys, you are doing important work, do not let some fool take you off your course. You are on a holy mission.

We all are shaken now and then by unfair criticism. Stay Strong.

Stay above it, remain true to yourself. Remember who you are.

# Honor Among Thieves
SEPTEMBER 21, 2015, ISRAEL

My dad grew up in Brooklyn, a different era, different times. It was before the State of Israel, before Jews could attend any club or college that they wanted, and then the Holocaust took place. My dad admired the Tough Jews, Jews who would not be pushed around, even though some were gangsters.

The same was true for the Italians and the Irish. That's how it was. When a famous gangster died the community mourned. The gangsters provided work, opportunities and a chance to break into the American life denied them.

Of course most Jews, Italians and Irish worked very hard under horrible conditions and upheld the law. They lived in rat infested tenements and raised children who would become honest Americans. None of these cultures condoned violence. Many gangsters such as Al Capone came from devoutly religious families.

Few things in life are as black and white as we originally think. There were two brothers in Boston, one "good" and one "bad". The good one was a politician, the bad one was a gangster and a killer. As it turns out they worked together, they were very close and the lines were blurred. The gangster made sure his brother got the votes he needed to stay in power. The politician made sure his brother was protected and well informed of police activities. Key witnesses mysteriously disappeared. Both escaped justice for decades.

So who is good and who is bad? Whom can you trust?

During World War Two the US government could not control the docks; Nazi infiltrators were coming in. They turned to the only ones who could control the docks, the Mafia, the Mob.

The CIA turned to the Italian Mafia to try and overthrow the Castro government in Cuba. And then Bobby Kennedy tries to destroy the Mob.

Use 'em when you need 'em and then dumb them when you don't?

So who is good and who is bad. Whom can you trust?

One thing my dad of blessed memory always stressed was honesty and honoring a deal. Sometimes we promise to do something, sometimes we make a commitment and then, things change. Honoring the deal will not benefit us right now, it will inconvenience us and cost us money. We made a mistake and now we must pay for it. *Rebbe gelt*, my dad said in Yiddish, learning money; School of Hard Knock's.

Once my dad met the legendary Jewish gangster, Mayer Lansky, in Tel Aviv. Lansky was deported by our prime minister. Israel did not allow an old Jew to return to his homeland. They feared his reputation with the Mafia. Not long ago an Israeli president went to prison as he was convicted of many crimes, including working with Israeli organized crime.

Who is good and who is bad? The lines are often blurred.

But honor a deal. A man must honor a deal.

Legend has it (actually more than just legend) that the notorious anti-Semite Joe Kennedy was deep in with the mob. He used these connections to get rich and to put his son into the greatest office in America, the presidency, but... for a price. The price was to go easy on the mob. You don't bite the hand that feeds you. JFK appoints his brother RFK, Bobby Kennedy to U.S. Attorney General. RFK declares war on the mob, on organized crime.

Eventually both brothers are assassinated. Officially no one knows the reason. Unofficially, a deal was not honored. And among thieves there is honor. While the killer of RFK said he did it because of the senator's "support of Israel" the case of JFK is less clear. Let's just say...in the words of Giancana's daughter, *"You don't bite the hand that feeds you, the Kennedy's bit the hand that fed them."* She said with anger and conviction. We get it.

Chicago mobster, Sam Giancana, was high on Robert Kennedy's hit list, and he was well aware of it.

Salvatore, "Sam", Giancana and other mobsters had been angered by the president's brother, Robert, who as U.S. attorney general was targeting organized crime in a major prosecution effort. A deal must be honored and if not, there is a price that must be paid.

### Honor a Deal

In 1992 the nephew of Sam Giancana published *Double Cross: The Story of the Man Who Controlled America.* The book attempted to establish that Giancana had rigged the 1960 Presidential election vote in Cook County, Chicago, on John Kennedy's behalf, which effectively gave Kennedy the election. It is argued that Kennedy reneged on the deal and therefore Giancana had him killed.

"It was then that Carlos Marcello's voice lost its softness, and his words were bitten off and spit out when mention was made of U.S. Attorney General Robert Kennedy, who was still on the trail of Marcello. *"Levarsi una pietra dalla scarpa!"* Carlos shrilled the cry of revenge: "Take the stone out of my shoe!"

A Sicilian knows what this means, get rid of the problem.

*"Don't worry about that little Bobby, son of a bitch,"* he shouted. *"He's going to be taken care of!"* Ever since Robert Kennedy had arranged for his deportation to Guatemala, Carlos had wanted revenge. But as the subsequent conversation, which was reported to two top Government investigators by one of the participants and later to this author, showed, he knew that to rid himself of Robert Kennedy he would first have to remove the President. Any killer of the Attorney General would be hunted down by his brother; the death of the President would seal the fate of his Attorney General.

No one at the meeting had any doubt about Marcello's intentions when he abruptly arose from the table. Marcello did not joke about such things. In any case, the matter had gone beyond mere "business"; it had become an affair of honor, a Sicilian vendetta."

# Easy Money
### September 22, 2015

Easy money.

*You think nobody knows how this feels*

I remember my college days, the music of Rickie Lee Jones, Easy Money. *There ain't no such thing as easy money*. And yet, people are always trying to convince us that there is a way to get easy money. Often we give ourselves "discounts" but that doesn't work, we just fool ourselves.

There ain't no such thing as easy money. There are high stakes, there are prison terms and shootings but there ain't no such thing as easy money.

Someone is always trying to tempt you into some great deal, some inside scoop. *Someone leaning on the back door...easy money.*

Shady characters, we have them in the martial arts world as well...easy money..easy ranks. Print up your own diplomas; buy some old camouflage uniform at the army surplus store....

*She says...Baby you can trust me, Baby it must be...*

*Now the dealer set the bet ...but he was wise to all of her lies.*

No such thing as easy ranks unless you are slow in the head, there ain't no such thing as easy ranks...

So I am looking at all the e mails sent to the IKI website over the past month and wondering why none of them joined us, why none of them sent in their payments for membership?

Made me think of this song, easy money. And my answer to them was no such thing, not with us.

So they send me a list of all their ranks, their training, drop a few names, tell me they are opening a school and need a rank. They try and impress me with what they did in the past...and they want an easy rank. *Ain't no such thing*, not with us. Some try to bribe me with a lucrative deal that includes giving them a black belt, fast.

I know everyone else is doing it, but we will not. If you train you earn rank. You leave IKI you leave your rank behind, because you are no longer training with us. If you retire you can keep your rank, you earned it.

We are for real, and really, there is no easy money and no easy rank.

And more reality, we grow old, and we need techniques based on wisdom. So don't send me video clips of hot Israeli girls with long hair in the IDF looking really cool. Video trash; has nothing to do with our reality. It is marketing garbage, nothing more.

But a smile and a kind word never grow old.

# Feeling Proud

September 24, 2015, El Al Business lounge, Ben Gurion Airport, Israel

Sitting in the business lounge in Israel's beautiful airport I feel proud of many things. I feel proud that Israel has a world class airport. It is named for our first prime minister, David Ben Gurion, who had a dream, and that dream has largely been fulfilled. Through hard work, idealism, and dedication, we have built a country we can be proud of.

I feel proud that I am sitting here. Thirty years ago I was asked to teach a small group of kids in the neighborhood; Naftali, Shaviv, Avi, Zvi, Aryeh and soon the first girl, Bat Sheva. Today, so many years later, I am a 6th *dan* black belt, internationally recognized with an international following. I have reason to be proud.

I have trained US Special Forces and Ukrainian national guards, German commandos, pilots and flight attendants, but that is not what this blog is about.

It is about a radio talk show I heard on the way to the airport today, which truly made me proud of Israel.

Israelis have always been known as blunt, uncouth, in your face. There is a certain honesty to this but over the years we have learned to be a little more polite, while still being blunt.

There was, as always, a heated political debate on the radio; Accusations of corruption, favoritism, etc.

And the host, this wise woman, says... *"There is room for legitimate disagreement. There is room for legitimate political differences, but there is no room for name calling or insults. We can conduct ourselves in a civil way."*

She elaborated on the difference between exposing poor performance on the job and name calling. The difference between courteous and fair legitimate disagreement on politics, and mudslinging in an attempt to discredit someone without actually proving he did anything wrong.

When one man severely criticized another she said, *"Have you ever actually met him?"*

I was inspired.

Now we have to make the same mature adjustment, adopt the same growing process in the Krav Maga world in particular and in the martial arts world in general.

I experienced that years ago at Dr. Jerry Beasley's Karate College, a true camaraderie of martial artists ranging from point sport Karate to Full contact MMA, all were respected.

I truly believe in our techniques but that does not mean I do not see other legitimate styles. Either way, I respect sincere people who really want to help others. We can always debate our differences of opinion.

IKI is proud to be a recognized world leader in Krav Maga and a member of the brotherhood of decent martial artists.

# Krav Maga Control and Goals

SEPTEMBER 25, 2015, GERMANY

We watch world events and sometimes we wonder; who is leading and who is being led? Often it is not clear.

A real man is in control, of his actions, his behavior, and his decisions. The weaker man is lead by others. Others set the tone, make the rules, and he follows.

Let us take a look at an imaginary scene. You are going out for a nice dinner with your girlfriend. Perhaps tonight will be the night you propose to her. Or, for our older readers; you are going out for your tenth anniversary, or fiftieth, it will be a special evening.

Now let's take a look at your goals for this evening

You want to impress your woman.

You want to have a wonderful evening, good food, wine, romance.

You want to share a special conversation, some laughs and smiles.

A man walks over to the two of you and begins to taunt you. He looks at your woman and says, *"Why waste your time with that loser! Don't you want to be with a real man?*

At first you are stunned by this behavior. And then the Bully continues with his taunts, he challenges: *"I am a real man, he is a flake, come with me and I will show you a good time"*

How do you react?

Do you accept his challenge and engage him in a fight?

Let's imagine for a moment that we live in the movies. It will play out like this. You accept his "manly" challenge, as any good Neanderthal should. You quickly beat him to a pulp.

If we are imagining a boxing movie, you finish him off with a couple of rapid-fire jabs and a hook. If you are Bruce Lee add a couple of high back spinning kicks. Chuck Norris, a slow simple side kick that totally knocks him out, Steven Segal, grab him and lock him up in an Akido lock, Adam Sandler, *The Zohan,* tie him up like a pretzel.

But as we say in Israel *Ata chai be seret*, you are living in a movie.

Now back to reality.

You get into a scuffle, you hit him, he hits you, whatever. Your woman is looking at you and trying to figure out why she was ever so foolish to ever pick you. The door seems like a better choice for her now. She would rather be with a true adult, not an immature adolescent.

So let's look at what happened to your perfect evening.

You got into a fight

You look like crap

You showed your woman that you have a short fuse and can easily snap and be dragged into a fight at any moment

You had no dinner

Now let's compare that to your original goals for the evening, are they the same?

No. They are not the same, not at all.

What happened is you were weak in character and you allowed someone to determine the course of events for you. You allowed someone with negative energy to draw you into his circle, into his bad negative energy.

His energy, his bad will, prevailed over yours. You lost as soon as you gave him that power.

You felt threatened, your ego was bruised and you felt a need to respond. Imagine you are a champion fighter and some kid writes that you are a coward and a loser, do you feel a need to get on a plane, meet him some place and "have it out" with him?

Is this a sign of maturity?

You know how many people insult our political leaders on a daily, hourly basis, and yet they never respond? Should they drop their important work of state to respond to some kid who thinks they "do not know how to do their job"?

We all know the answer to that. So perhaps we should think about that in our own lives.

A rabbi once said "I choose my friends, and I choose my enemies, I did not choose you for either" and he walked away. Yes, he walked away. At that moment in my eyes he stood 10 feet tall and was the greatest fighter I had ever seen.

# The Best Defense

SEPTEMBER 28, 2015, KÖNIGSBACH, GERMANY

Many instructors claim that they will teach you the best defense. Everyone else is teaching nonsense, techniques that will get you killed, but they, and only they, have the best defense. Ignore the rest and go to the best. They guarantee your success.

No one can guarantee anything.

While no one can guarantee with absolute certainty what will work, we do try our best. Our techniques are designed to be as simple as possible. We avoid any complicated motions. We avoid anything that involves the need for memory, muscle, speed or great skill. Our aim is to only use techniques that are:

*Easy to learn*

*Easy to apply in many diverse situations*

*Easy to remember under stress*

We feel we have provided a great service in this way, and we have had countless testimonies of how our techniques have been successfully employed in real life situations. In some cases the successful defender had only attended one seminar, or just a few classes.

However, there is a better defense.

While guns can defend us, to some extent, the only true defense is peace. So we follow the example of our forefather Jacob, and the Biblical directive, to pray and work for peace while also preparing for war.

We are not fools of course: war, murder, and violence have always been part of the human condition and at this point things are only getting worse. However, if you can make a friend you can save some bullets. While we will certainly never eliminate all of our enemies we must always attempt to make as many true friends as possible. When you have made a friend you have eliminated an enemy.

There is more than one way to eliminate an enemy.

People who create many enemies, such as professional gangsters, tend to live shorter lives despite having better protection than most of us. The best ultimate defense is to make more friends.

But we never stop training. Hope for the best, prepare for the worst. Work for peace but prepare for war.

### *The IKI Mission*

The IKI mission is the ultimate goal of all martial arts systems, all Krav Maga systems; to live in peace. As such a big part of IKI activities is to spread peace among all peoples.

We are not naive but we do believe that every time one person extends his hand in peace to another we are taking another step towards a more peaceful world.

Already I have seen with my own eyes incredible results. Via my Krav Maga tours around the world I have come into contact with many diverse groups of people who had never previously had any in-depth contact with a Jew from Israel.

Via our Tour and Train Israel program I have brought hundreds of foreign students to Israel, they have experienced Israel and Israel has experienced them.

I know that in my own community this has been a huge difference in terms of breaking down barriers and rethinking stereotypes. In my own life and in the lives of others I have seen monumental changes.

What we stand for as human beings and what we teach as martial arts instructors must be in sync. We work for a better world.

# Organizational Planning
### SEPTEMBER 29, 2015, KÖNIGSBACH, GERMANY

Back in the days of Moses his devoted disciples felt he was not strict enough with the people. When Joshua felt that Eldad and Medad were acting out of line he turned to Moshe/Moses and said, *"Sir Moshe, lock them up"*. (Numbers, 11, 28)

Moses took a more lenient approach and let the matter go.

This raises the question, central power or delegation of power, absolute authority or freedom, what works best?

Hitler thought that in a moment of truth democracies would not be able to fight; only a dictatorship would work. The Soviets felt that any relaxation of power would lead to collapse.

How to maintain control over time? How to govern effectively while preventing revolution or a people's takeover?

With IKI there are those that like the idea of "The government that governs least governs best" (Henry David Thoreau, *Civil Disobedience*) while others would like to see me exercise greater control over members and keep them more in line with IKI philosophy.

I believe in keeping control and maintaining quality while also not stepping on people's toes. I want to allow instructors a measure of independence and yet maintain the IKI way. It is a delicate balance and to be honest it does not always work.

But there is no system of government that always works. Communists become Capitalists, become Fascists become Socialists...

I like what Albert Speer wrote about his position (in the Nazi leadership) as minister of Armaments. While others were fighting a war he and his associates were jockeying for personal power.

In his book he rarely deals with issues such as the Jews, genocide, enslavement of the Slavic nations etc., but focuses on himself and his power, with ... *"My injured self-esteem, the sense of having been personally offended..."* (337)

What he writes about his position and his attempts to maintain his position is insightful; he wrote the following to Hitler in 1944. Germany was losing the war; Speer was finally becoming more independent and felt he was free from the "suggestive powers" of Hitler. He wrote, *"I have always, even in the days when I was your architect, followed the rule of letting my assistants work independently. I grant that this principle has often brought me severe disappointments, for not everyone is worthy of such trust, and some men, after having acquired sufficient prestige, have been disloyal to me."*

*"Be this as it may, I will go on following this principle with iron consistency. In my view it is the only one that permits a man to govern and create. The higher the position, the more true it is."* (Inside the Third Reich, page 337)

With IKI the goal is not my personal power, or "controlling markets" but simply maintaining quality, unity and the purity of our goals. But no system of governing or leadership is perfect. As with Moses there will always be those who want more freedom and those who want more control. Too free and you have nothing, too tight and you suffocate people. Finding the balance is the key, and the challenge.

There will always be those who after a few ranks will feel they are fit to start and head their own Krav Maga association. Most will fail.

There will always be those who find fault and leave, many will regret this decision but will be ashamed to return.

And all leaders, as Albert Speer expressed, will have to deal with disappointments, it is the nature of the position.

So we do our best, and try to keep our balance while maintaining our purity and yet knowing we will make mistakes.

# My Friend Zack

October 1, 2015

*Zack and me, class photo, 1973, side by side.*

I do not know where this blog will take me. It has no particular goal or point, just a need to put pen to paper.

How the years fly by. 1969, a new kid in town, from Canada. I am a shy kid and my mother tells me to go over and introduce myself to this new guy in town. So I listen to my dear mother and do so.

I remember the clothing, the style, 1969. The music.

We become best friends; we hang out together all the time. We go to school together, take the bus home together. Adopt a puppy. Whenever I hear the song by the Beatles, ***"Two of Us"***, I think of Zack and me.

"Two of us riding nowhere..."

*"not arriving... on our way back home, we are our way home, we're going home"*

On weekends we snuck into construction sites to play, we hung out too late, we disappeared for hours on end. We did so many things. We played baseball, built a little "go cart", even got into a little trouble now and then. I remember when our little brothers got into a fight, we were punished together and had to write 100 times, "One must separate between brothers who quarrel"

"יש להפריד בן אחים רבים"

I have not forgotten that phrase, the punishment worked.

The years passed, we moved in different directions. But at university we were back together. Goodness, the memories come back and overwhelm me. I remember when this girl wanted to go out with him...

*"You and I have memories longer than the road that stretches out of here..."*

She told me to be subtle. Subtle? With my lifelong friend? I just went up and said, *"Zack, Amy is crazy about you, she wants to go out."*

One is not subtle with such friends.

Memories...summer camp with lousy food, my band playing a party at his big house, girlfriends, You and me chasing paper getting nowhere on our way back home, we're on our way home...

Zack, the years disappear. On our way back home...

and now he is going home. I miss you my friend.

Zack moved back to Canada, had a family, five kids. We kind of lost touch. Saw him now and then when he came to Israel. We kept in touch now and then. And then he was hit with something, he described it as a bolt of lightning going through his head. Surgery, recovery, treatment...Zack fought on.

A few months ago an old friend, Stewart, part of our little gang, wrote me that Zack was in a hospice. I began calling weekly. At first he could talk a little. Nechama, his wife, said his spirits were lifted whenever he heard my voice. This made me so happy. She said it made him smile.

We relived childhood memories. I said out loud, *Zack old buddy I love you*. So important to say these things. And I truly mean it.

I flew to Germany for a Krav Maga seminar. My brother wrote me that he had heard from Amiel, another childhood friend living in Canada, that Zack was near the end. But he held on. Amiel wrote that Zack truly desired life, and that every day was precious to him. How sweet and profound.

Nechama told me how *"Zack had a good day, Zack is eating, Zack enjoyed being outside in the nice weather."*

He loved life and appreciated every day.

What a lesson for us.

I can picture him, lying in bed, no hope for recovery, but smiling because an old friend is on the phone from Israel.

Old friends...on our way back home. We are on our way home, we're going home. You and I have memories...

How fast life goes by. And I can picture his house way back when... and I can hear his voice.

I had hoped that Zack would hold on a little bit longer, so I could call one more time, at least. I spoke to him when I was in California, with my brother Michael, we both spoke with him, our dear friend. That was like a little reunion.

To lose such a friend is to lose another part of myself. Zack passed away just a couple of days ago. He passed away on the first morning of Sukkoth, the Feat of Tabernacles. I can still see in my memory the Sukkah, the hut, at Zack's home, which was always open and welcoming.

He is gone now, and I could not attend the funeral. And I am sad.

Zack was a good guy. He was not a world champion in anything, not brilliant, not an inventor, but a solid good guy. He smiled, he laughed, he was modest and honest. He was my friend and I miss him.

# Krav Maga and the Mona Lisa

OCTOBER 2, 2015

I am not an artist and to be honest I have little appreciation for art. I look at a painting, looks nice, great, let's move on. I am not one of those who can spend hours in an art gallery. I cannot spend an hour looking at a painting and finding the hidden meaning behind it.

I am full of admiration for those who do possess this deep appreciation of art, but I am not gifted in that way. My point is that this lack of appreciation is no reflection on the art or the artist, only on the viewer, in this case - me. In an art gallery I will be looking for the coffee shop.

If an artist spends a year on a painting and I look at it and do not see the greatness in it, he should not feel bad; this is no reflection on him or his art, only on an uneducated viewer.

It takes a certain level of knowledge and training to appreciate a work of art, any work of art.

I recall in college, arguing with ignorant Jews about the Talmud. These people studied a few pages (in translation) or read an article and felt they could argue with the great rabbis of antiquity. They challenged the words of our sages and felt they had a right to do so. I recall their foolish words, "Why can't another voice join this great discussion?" "Rabbi Hillel has his opinion and so do I", said some girl at UCLA.

Well, let's think about it. Hillel spent forty years studying night and day before expressing his opinion. You read an article.

Perhaps I should join a group of professors discussing Quantum Physics and express my thoughts? Perhaps I should argue with them and point out their faults? I can't even join a discussion with teenagers about the latest cell phone or tablet!

You need knowledge and experience before joining any discussion. I disagree with the idea that everyone has a right to their opinion. Everyone has a right to study and those who understand a topic have a right to their opinion.

Better to remain quiet and be thought a fool then to open your mouth and erase all doubt.

Just look at some of the beauty queen contestants! They are mostly brain dead women who can't answer any of the questions intelligently. So why bother asking them questions? Just judge them the way you would judge a dog show.

And the same is true of martial arts and Krav Maga.

Bruce Lee often said he does not want to train anyone unless they had already attained a black belt in at least one style. He wanted to train educated people who could appreciate what he was teaching.

After years of training I can understand him. Police officers, soldiers, martial arts instructors quickly understand what I am showing them. But sometimes eighteen-year-old boys from privileged backgrounds challenge me. They think they know better, they think they should point out what I am doing wrong and educate me as to the errors of my way. We have a word for this; *Hutzpah,* arrogance without limits. It is an old Yiddish word derived from Hebrew, derived from ancient Aramaic.

It means: Unmitigated effrontery or impudence; gall. Audacity; nerve, the trait of being rude and impertinent; inclined to take liberties. In Hebrew, *chutzpah* is used indignantly, to describe someone who has overstepped the boundaries of accepted behavior.

So how does this fit in with Krav Maga?

On one hand we say question everything. This is your life and you have a right to the very best defense. On the other hand we have the Mr. Miyagi wisdom, teacher say - student do. No questions.

Both are true.

As with the Talmudic scholars, a beginner has a right to ask questions. If something does not make sense, ask, speak up. Sometimes a beginner will offer a new perspective. But do so with the appropriate respect. You are speaking to a rabbi, a man who has earned his title.

I recall as a young student in university, UCLA. Studying the "light" topic of Jewish mysticism, I asked a question without the appropriate respect for the knowledge of the teacher. He was self defined as "secular" although he grew up Orthodox, and I questioned his understanding of religion. When I felt he did not get what I was saying I restated my question. To this day I recall his wise answer, *"Young man, you do not need to clarify your opinion, I grew up with your opinion, I understand it better than you do."*

Thirty plus years later I know he was right. Thank you Professor Amos Funkenstein.

Respect earned.

So on one hand we say like Mr. Miyagi, no questions, on the other hand we say question everything. The apparent contradiction is resolved by common sense. First learn, train, gain some understanding. If you do not understand by all means ask! But do so with humility. Understand that the person standing in front of you has already dealt with that question. He already thought of that issue himself and has a reason for doing what he is doing, the way he is doing it. Do not assume that you have found something he never thought of. Show some respect for his training.

When you reach a higher level, a much higher level, you will be able to have your own opinion. Knowledge and wisdom take time to attain.

So if you cannot appreciate the Mona Lisa, please do not assume that all these years all the great experts were simply mistaken. Assume they see something that you cannot see yet.

**Footnote:** Having not thought of my dear professor for some time I decided to search for him. Sadly I discovered that he passed away at an early age, 58, from cancer. I recall that he was a heavy smoker. In those days one was allowed to smoke in class. Once when he ran out of cigarettes he took a break and went to his car to get more.

As bright as he was he fell victim to the smoking addiction.

I was sad to learn that his life ended so soon. Reading about him I discovered that I was correct, I was studying with a true genius.

For more than three decades I have not forgotten his name, his expressions, or his lessons. Now I realize he was indeed a rare genius. I feel privileged to have been his student. And although I disagree with him on nearly every aspect of religion and politics, I deeply respect him.

From 1995

### Renaissance man' Amos Funkenstein dies at age 58

Called a genius and Renaissance man by his academic colleagues, Amos Funkenstein was known for reciting long passages verbatim in Latin, German and Greek decades after reading them.

Winner of the coveted Israel Prize for History, the U.C. Berkeley history professor could lecture effortlessly on nearly any element of Jewish or non-Jewish civilization from the biblical period through the 20th century.

Raised an Orthodox Jew in pre-state Israel, he was considered the quintessential *apikoros* - a heretic who knew the tradition inside and out, yet rejected any belief in its divine origin.

Funkenstein died Saturday, Nov. 11 in Berkeley after a yearlong battle with cancer. He was 58.

"He was truly a Renaissance man in terms of intellectual interest," said Professor David Biale, "He was probably the only genius I've ever met."

Considered rare even among world-class academics for his intellectual abilities, Funkenstein was primarily a historian of Judaism, medieval intellectualism and science.

He authored seven books and more than 50 articles, writing in German, Hebrew, English and French. His books included "Perceptions of Jewish History," "Theology and the Scientific Imagination from the Middle Ages to the Seventeenth Century," and "Sociology of Ignorance," which he wrote with childhood friend Rabbi Adin Steinsaltz. At the time of his death, he was working on a multi-volume study of the social and cultural context of knowledge in Western history since antiquity.

Educated in a religious school in Jerusalem, Funkenstein served in the Israeli army and then studied for two years at the Hebrew University of Jerusalem before transferring to the Free University of Berlin in the late 1950s. In 1967, he was hired to teach at UCLA...

Funkenstein could offer detailed critiques of books he had read 20 years earlier, Biale recalled, and he would doodle mathematical proofs for fun.

"He had a photographic memory," Biale said. But even this ability was just intellectual pyrotechnics. "What counted with him was originality."

Unlike many of his peers in academia, Funkenstein rejected much of the formality associated with the job. He wanted students to call him by his first name and became friends with many of them.

In the late 1970s while still at UCLA, Funkenstein began teaching part of the year at Tel Aviv University, where he held an endowed chair in history and the philosophy of science.

# Zuz

### October 2, 2015, Israel

For anyone who served in the Israeli Defense Forces the term "Zuz" is well known. It means "Move". As in - here is the assignment; you have 7 minutes to complete it, Zuz!

And you move!

There is no time to think, to analyze, to debate, to question. You just move. And so it is in life.

We think too much. We over analyze and we paralyze ourselves. Of course we need to think about our actions, of course we do need to analyze. Fools rush in where angels fear to tread. We must seek a balance and be cautious.

But some of us are too cautious. We look at our options and we think, and think, and double think. And then it is too late, the opportunity has gone. And then we wonder why we do not get any breaks in life. Sometimes the breaks come but we are too busy thinking. Sometimes we just need to act, to hear our commander shout Zuz! and just go.

We must not let opportunities slip away.

So when we get stuck in a rut, we must remember Zuz! Move, get out of where you are, do something, anything!

In self-defense the worst thing you can do is to do nothing. At a certain point, after quickly taking in all available facts, you make a decision and you act. Zuz!

# First Line of Defense

October 3, 2015, Israel

We have a wonderful police force here in Israel. We are very proud of them and they do an amazing job.

But that is not enough. Not here, not anywhere. The secret service, the military, the air-force, the police, they can all do their job perfectly but it is still not enough. We need you.

You and I are the first line of defense.

Tonight we were attacked again. The perpetrators have not been arrested; they have been shot on the spot. Police reacted immediately. Some of the attackers are in the hospital now, others are dead.

Our police care and are doing their job. But it is not enough.

We need you. But you ...need training.

Sadly two of our people are dead, others are struggling for their lives. I wish some had struggled with their attackers, but they did not. I am not looking to find fault, I am looking to find lessons; Lessons for us so we can survive.

One of the dead had a handgun. In fact that is why he was chosen, the attacker stabbed him and took his gun. The attacker tried to shoot more people but missed. The real damage was caused by the knife.

The deaths were caused by the stabbings, not the shootings. The police did their job and the entire incident was over in less than two minutes.

Israel is safe because we have police everywhere, there was police 50 meters from the attack and he shot and killed the Arab attacker at one. He did his job well.

*A police spokesperson said the attacker, 19-year-old Mohand Halabi from Ramallah, first stabbed the father of the baby and took his gun, which he used to fire at group of nearby tourists until he was neutralized.* (Ynet news)

This father is dead now. His 22-year-old wife is in the hospital. The baby will never know his father.

People like to feel there is always a big daddy that will take care of us, that we really do not need to worry or take action on our own. This is a badly sadly mistaken notion. We must take matters into our own hands.

Let's look at this incidence and see what we can learn from it.

The attacker was not a Rambo looking type. When I teach Krav Maga I get questions that imply that we are dealing with super human SWAT guys gone bad. In fact most attackers are like this guy, a meek weak looking skinny 19 year old kid. He looked so meek I would not even want him for a sparring partner.

We must train in Krav Maga; we must practice the basics again and again. We must learn our knife defenses.

We must teach and practice situational awareness.

We must always be alert in public places.

We must make time for Krav Maga training, no matter what. Our kids spend hours and hours each day in school learning material that they will mostly forget or never use, but there is no time for Krav Maga.

Students sign up for Krav Maga but "other obligations" come up and soon they find they have no time. As my father used to say, "The greatest waste of time is an early death". Train hard and do your best to avoid an early death. Someone needs you.

# Different ways of training in Krav Maga

OCTOBER 4, 2015, ISRAEL

It is well known that as much as we are all the same in some ways, we are also very different. There are no two people in the world with exactly the same face and body, even identical twins are not identical.

So it should come as no surprise that we all have different ways of learning. There are highly intelligent people who have great difficulty in learning a new language. There are brilliant people who have to overcome huge obstacles just to play basic sports or learn a martial art. We are all different.

Some can watch a video and mimic the technique exactly. Some can watch the video and fully grasp the technique and be able to apply it at once. Others need to hear the explanation while yet others need to feel the teachers' hand guiding their body in the correct direction.

Personally, tell me something and I will not get it, let me try it myself under your supervision, and I will totally understand.

Therefore when people ask if they can fully master a martial art by video the answer depends more on them then on me, or any instructor.

In this day and age we have the benefit of many new technologies that were unavailable in the past. In the past once the teacher was no longer with the students, arguments would develop. What did the teacher actually say? What did he mean? Today, at least in martial arts or Krav Maga training we can simply watch a DVD even if he is thousands of miles away, or...passed on to another life.

A good video/DVD will show the technique from several angles. My personal team of Baruch and Laizer will not allow me to be lazy. They insist on filming everything from several angels, including the foot work. They want to make sure that our long distance students can see what we are doing here in Israel.

# Social Media and Krav Maga
## October 7, 2015

Years ago I was teaching a basic Krav Maga seminar. We covered a great deal that seminar but we did not cover knife attacks. Only so much you can do in one seminar. As I was leaving someone said, "Hey, can you show me how to defend against a knife attack?"

Now, for all the instructors out there, that was the punch line, and surely now you are laughing but also crying a little.

Knife attacks are deadly. I have been training in knife defense for more than thirty years and I hope I never have to face a real blade. Respect the blade, the knife, the machete, the ax, for they are all deadly and unpredictable. You must train.

You cannot learn how to defend against a knife attack by asking a quick question as the instructor is leaving the room and expect that a brief answer will help you.

Krav Maga is indeed designed to be a short cut. It is designed to take less time to gain a decent level than other, more traditional, martial arts, but it still takes time.

A short cut is a short cut but it is not immediate. There may be a short cut from Chicago to New York but it will still take time. This is not instant miso soup.

So today some guy posts a question; there have been a few deadly knife attacks in Jerusalem recently and some people are showing signs of waking up. Some people are beginning to realize that at some point they may have to defend themselves.

But are they signing up for Krav Maga classes? No, they are posting questions on social media. So this person posts a question asking what is the best way to "ward off a knife attacker". The answers run from the ignorant to the absurd. The one thing most of them have in common is a complete and total lack of martial arts education. I.e. everyone feels free to offer advice, without actually having any knowledge of the topic at hand.

When I begin to discuss Krav Maga training the questioner becomes insulted. He was not looking for Krav Maga training; he was simply looking for some easy tips to avoid getting stabbed.

Easy tips? Wow. I am nearly speechless.

When I suggested Krav Maga training the person's reply was, *"If a dear friend called you up and was feeling very sick, would you tell them to go to medical school?"*

No, of course not, but there is a difference, the Krav Maga instructor cannot defend you, he cannot be there when you are attacked, but the doctor can heal you.

A thought entered my head; I want to build a house. So post on social media; anyone have any ideas how to make sure my house does not collapse? And someone might write in, Contact a building company. And my response - I am just looking for some advice!

Speechless. If I want to build a house, I must contact a builder, if I need medical advice I do not post on the internet, I contact a doctor. And if you want to learn to defend against a man hell bent upon stabbing you to death - For God's sake go train in Krav Maga!!

Even a shortcut takes time, even Krav Maga involves some effort and commitment.

There is no short cut home; there is no easy way out. It is time to face the music.

# Ask Questions

### October 8, 2015, Woodmere, NY, USA

Krav Maga Tour

There are many advantages to the Hi Tech age. One of them is that rather than just remembering things we can actually record them and listen back.

Wouldn't you like to hear Moses Speak? How about hear King David recite his Psalms?

The printing press was considered a great invention and innovation. Instead of having to copy a book by hand, now it became possible to print thousands of books. But the digital age has taken a step further. Now you can hear the great master, even years after his death, in his own voice. Amazing.

However, it is still not enough. Our wise rabbis understood thousands of years ago that the key is not the written word, nor any recording, but personal interaction. In ancient Hebrew it was referred to as Serving the Master. Today we might call it "Paying your dues".

When I was a young guitar player the older guys always said....If you want to play the blues you got to pay your dues and you know it don't come easy"

I believe that song was written by Ringo Star and sung with the late great George Harrison.

You know it don't come easy...

You have to interact with your teacher. You have to watch him closely, and clarify any doubts. That is the Jewish way of learning. When I was in high school playing football we had a coach who didn't get that. He would shout out the orders, long, short, cut across. I would say, "Excuse me coach, let me see if I got this straight, you want to run along this line, make a sharp left and then prepare to catch the ball?"

He would look at the other players and say, "What is wrong with this guy, is he stupid?"

They responded, "Actually no, he is one of the best students in the school, he is just very thorough, he wants to make sure he understands it correctly."

I ask questions, I never assume I got it right the first time, I assume there is more than meets the eye, I want to read between the lines. I clarify the matter until there is no doubt. Other people just give up, or assume it just does not make sense.

With Krav Maga we have the advantage these days of DVDs and on-line video training, but it is not enough for most people. When I arrive to teach my seminars I find that many are making small but important mistakes. This includes instructors. That is why I travel.

Receiving the video clips is great, but not often it is not enough. Having the clips is like reading the required text books in college. You still need the professor to elucidate, elaborate and make sense of it all. Otherwise just buy the book and skip college.

If you watch the video clip and you "don't see it", ASK.

There are basically three options; either I do not know what I am doing, you are missing something, or you stumbled across something that no one else has pointed out to me in thirty years.

Today one wise student came up with two excellent questions. We are always open to exploring new situations. There is hardly a seminar without some great questions and a few new innovations.

Where else do you see new techniques being developed live?

We are open to questions, but please, do not take a look at a video clip, and assume "it does not work". Be a little bit humble and assume that perhaps you may have missed something. Perhaps another video clip is on its way with a better angle that will clarify your doubts.

And remember, it don't come easy, you need to ask questions.

# Rapid Cure
OCTOBER 12, 2015, RINCON, PUERTO RICO

Over the past week Israel has experienced an eruption of attacks from our Arab neighbors, this has been the case for the past 1,400 years. It has nothing to do with local politics or our actions. There have always been attacks and each time the local Village Fools, i.e. the politicians, attempt to offer reasons and explanations for this behavior. It is because Jews visited the Holy Temple Mount, it is because Jews choose to live exactly where their ancestors are buried, it is because Jews choose to live among gentiles...etc...

It does not matter.

After each spate of attacks requests for Krav Maga lessons pop up like mushrooms after a storm. And they disappear as quickly as well. Some young instructors get excited, they think that now everyone sees the need for Krav Maga and will sign up for classes and make a solid commitment. They begin to plan their schedules to make room for this huge influx of students. They plan to rent a bigger training hall...Oh... the young and naive.

Sadly the human condition does not really change at all. Yesterday's headlines are tomorrow's headlines. Such is life.

But we still work hard, for the few who will listen. And we hope, we pray, we plan. We prepare. For maybe a few will wise up.

Dr. Herzl had a dream of a Jewish state where Jews would be free from the persecution of the gentiles, (Christian, Muslim, Atheists, whatever, I think we have never had any trouble from the Buddhists).

Of course he was an idealist, and of course most people mocked him. Yet his dream was so great that even an early death could not defeat him. When Herzl came home he wrote in his diary that fifty years from today a Jewish state will rise again. The year was 1897. In the year 1948 the new, reborn, third commonwealth of the Jewish nation came into being. Dear Dr. Herzl was off by only one year. Not bad for a modern day secular prophet.

But he was followed only by very few in his lifetime. Just as today, the majority of those who would benefit by his actions refused to lift a finger.

I can imagine that after every Pogrom, when the locals came into the Jewish community to rape, kill, smash and burn, voices were heard calling for mass immigration to the land of Israel and rebuilding our own land. However, then as now, as soon as things calmed down the zeal of those mushrooms after the storm also calmed down.

And people like Dr. Herzl once again stood alone.

And so it is today. Four Jews murdered in one weekend, many more attacked and hurt, and the cries come out for more Krav Maga instructors. But do not worry, there is little need.

One inquirer wanted a onetime session to learn to defend herself and her family. Really, can I learn Swedish in a onetime session?

Another asked how many lessons does one need; I asked how many times does one need to eat? It is the same.

Imagine an angry, frustrated, religiously motivated hard core killer coming at you. Remember these are people who decapitate others, it is no longer a secret. We have seen them do this. And these hardened killers are coming at you, at a time and place that you do not suspect and you are armed with...."How many lessons do I need?"

Are you kidding me?

Imagine you are going undercover to an Arab country and you ask, how many lessons in Arabic do I need?

Your life is at stake and you are playing games. You are looking for a quick cure. Well....sorry to disappoint you. No such thing exists.

So for all those newbie instructors making grandiose plans to accommodate all their new students...get a good novel to fill that time.

As soon as the storm passes, so will their interest and motivation.

I recall when I started my martial arts training a wiser and older student told me that I am one in a thousand. It took me a while to understand. This was a warning. Do not expect too much, only one in a thousand has my level of motivation.

But I am here, as is my staff, and we are motivated to help you, but you must get yourself in the door first. You must make a move.

# Krav Maga Joy
OCTOBER 13, 2015, RINCON, PUERTO RICO

Krav Maga Tour

We have an expression in Hebrew, the teacher is licking honey. Well to be honest that is not always the case. Managing Krav Maga schools all over the world it is often difficult to maintain quality control. When the cat is away the mouse will play.

To be fair it is not always easy for the local instructors to get all the techniques correct. We have our annual seminars, our training in Israel, our up to date DVDs and our On-Line program. We do everything we can to keep our instructors totally up to date with all the latest Krav Maga developments and innovations. But sometimes it is not enough.

Sometimes, sadly, the teacher is not licking honey but eating dust. I show up to teach a seminar and the local students look helpless. They do not know what I am teaching, it looks new to them, they seem unfamiliar with the techniques.

Some of them do not even know that I send out daily video clip updates. Sometimes, I show a technique, and a student will say, "That is so much easier and more effective than what our instructor is teaching". That is not a good sign.

One student came to Israel after training in Krav Maga for three years. When he saw what we were really teaching he quit his instructor. He felt bitter, angry, and deceived; the instructor was claiming to be an IKI instructor but in fact was teaching sometime else.

Not every member teaches exactly what we teach. Not every member claims to. Some bring their own valuable experience into their game. What saddens me is when techniques are transferred incorrectly, with mistakes. The student never gets the full benefit of what we have to offer. When I see this it is like the old game "telephone" where one child starts with a word but by the time it reaches the tenth child it is something totally different, unrecognizable from the original intent.

And then there are the good days. Last night I thought the regular class of IKI Black Belt Instructor Jorge Castillo. It was a pleasure. I introduced some new situations that they had not previously dealt with. So it was all new. But yet it was not all new.

They picked up all the new material incredibly fast, but the reason was obvious. Their instructor, Jorge, had carefully laid the ground work. In IKI we stress the concept, once you correctly understand the concept the rest is easy. You can apply this concept easily to an infinite number of situations. And that is exactly what happened here. It was a pleasure, I showed a technique, they recognized the concept, and they did it correctly the first time.

Now the instructor is licking honey. Actually I am having day old coffee but it tastes sweet to me; the joys of being a teacher.

I am thankful for instructors like Jorge Castillo, in so many ways. And his students are most fortunate.

He truly grasps the IKI way. Everything being taught here in Puerto Rico is identical to what we are teaching back home in Israel. Nothing is lost in translation, a proud moment for all of us.

# Kadima ~ Forward
### October 22, 2015, Pensacola, Florida, USA

Krav Maga Tour

Touring the world and teaching Krav Maga I try my best to impart a little of the spirit of Krav Maga, the spirit of Israel and the Jewish people. This is the spirit behind all we do, and it permeates every technique and strategy. We are taking the bitter lessons of our people, our experience, and sharing it with the world in an attempt to help people cope with violence and everyday life.

Krav Maga is not only about physical violence, it is about coping with life. Sometimes life can hit us harder than any opponent.

Last night I taught a seminar and among the many women in the group were some who had experienced physical and emotional abuse for many years. Some could not even stay for the entire seminar; the thought of the abuse was too much.

Teaching the physical techniques is important but it is not enough. For some the very sight of a rubber training knife or gun is enough to cause anxiety. These fears and trauma are real and we must deal with them.

But to all these things we say Kadima, Forward!

Imagine an entire nation traumatized. Imagine a nation on the brink of destruction coming back to life, from the hell and gas chambers of Europe to the fire and brimstone of hatred in the Middle East. How many families do I know where the grandfather was killed by the Nazis and their associates, and the grandson, named for the martyred grandfather, was killed in the line of duty protecting Israel from its enemies that surround her.

Yes, I know many. And yet we came home and moved forward, Kadima. We move forward because there is no other option. Backwards does not exist for us.

We move forward because backwards are the trains headed for Auschwitz, Treblinka and Sobibor, our families have been on those trains. If you think those trains exist only in the past you are delusional. There are those ready to get the engines started. They are waiting…

So we have no way to go back. We are a small people and a very small country. On all sides are enemies except for one side where we have the sea. Our enemies have a slogan; Throw the Jews into the sea.

We have nowhere to go but forward.

So when life hits hard we look straight into the storm and say…. We have survived Pharaoh of Egypt we shall survive this too. We say you have no idea what this nation is made of. We shall build an iron wall out of straw if we must but we shall not retreat.

Forward, Kadima is our only direction.

Kadima is an attitude, a forward moving attitude. But this does not mean a strict policy of combat. In our style of Krav Maga we do advocate a forward movement all the time however at a certain point, depending upon the situation; we also advocate a strategic retreat.

We do not advocate the Hitler philosophy of never retreating, this policy unnecessarily led to the loss of hundreds of thousands of German soldiers; kids sacrificed for a bizarre ideology. For us there is a time to take a small step backwards and regroup. Constant forward motion could be suicide. With Krav Maga we advocate APC; Ability, Purpose, Circumstance to determine how to finish every technique. There is a time to continue forward and a time to get strike and get away.

So while our philosophy is always forward we must not confuse this with blind moving into enemy territory. Fools rush in where angels fear to tread.

Kadima is the attitude of never giving up. Kadima is taking a step in the right direction, despite pain and trauma. And Kadima is used a great deal in our Krav Maga approach.

# Understand the Student
October 23, 2015, Atlanta airport, USA

Krav Maga Tour

In most teaching environments, the emphasis is on understanding the material, understanding the teacher, the instructor. This is how it was for me in college and in most or all courses I ever took.

The grand professor walks in, high and mighty, you should feel privileged to be allowed in his class, and now…you must prove yourself.

He will speak in high tones, at his own pace, it is your job to keep up. You are told that many will not complete the course, this is a warning: Pay attention or you will be out.

What a great method of education. The strong will survive, the weak will be weeded out.

It all depends on your goals, to find potential world champions, or secret agents, or SWAT team members, or train regular folks.

It is our goal to train everyone. We want to find the lowest common denominator, techniques that will work for as many people as possible, and an approach that will reach as many people as possible.

If you are designing airline safety equipment for passengers you want something that everyone will be able to use, not only the commando soldiers.

When looking at our students we need to see not only their strengths but also their weaknesses. We must understand their challenges, emotional and physical and work with that.

If someone has been traumatized by a knife threat we don't have fun by randomly running up to them with a rubber training knife. Each topic must be addressed in a sensitive way.

Many Krav Maga schools pride themselves on being scary, tough guys, bully types. We do not.

We pride ourselves on teaching everyone, kids, old people, victims of violent crimes. For these are the people that need us most.

In the USA we are approaching Halloween, you want to be scary? Put on a scary Halloween custom and get over it, but don't bring that to class. We are here to teach, not to scare.

# Krav Maga Quality Control

October 26, 2015, Windsor, Co, USA

Krav Maga Tour

I am on my Fall Krav Maga tour, traveling around the United States, teaching students and instructors, beginners and advanced.

I teach groups, but yet I must not see a group, I must see individuals. Each individual has his own needs and expectations. It is the art of observation and fine tuning. It is the art of knowing when to correct and how much, and when to let go.

It is exciting to introduce newcomers to Krav Maga, our style of Krav Maga, and see the look on the faces; Wow, this is simple! I can do it! It is also gratifying to see the true teachers. The true teachers always remain students.

Some students who view themselves as "advanced practitioners" will participate or watch a seminar and say.... same old stuff. They are so wrong it is sad. They will use this as an excuse not to attend a future seminar, feeling that they already know it all.

Yesterday I taught a seminar that I really enjoyed. Among the participants were those with ranks of master and high level black belts in various styles. But none were nonchalant; none had the attitude of "I know it all, there is nothing new to learn". Even with techniques which I have taught before they observed subtle points which they had not noticed before. The same was true with my seminars in other parts of the USA; guys with 4th dan in Karate, 5th dan in Hapkido, 6th dan in Kenpo, as well as black belts in Krav Maga opened their eyes with that Ah Ha look.

They told me that unresolved questions were answered, little points of difficulty resolved and new levels of understanding reached. This shows the true student and the true teacher. The one who thinks he knows it all will walk away with "same stuff as last year", and will have learned nothing while the true high level instructor will walk away with new insights and true progress.

That is part of the goal of these tours; to maintain our quality control of Krav Maga, to fix some bad habits that creep in while I am away, bad habits that can totally change the effect of the technique, to make sure that you are getting it right.

The open minded humble true martial artist will see this benefit, and say Ah Ha! Now I get it, while the one who thinks he knows it all will walk away feeling he wasted his time since "it is all the same stuff".

A little point can make all the difference in the understanding and performance of a technique. A word here or there can change everything. That is the job of the teacher. That is our Krav Maga quality control.

# The Price We Pay
October 29, 2015, Charlotte airport, North Carolina, USA

Krav Maga Fall Tour

The price we pay for our training...

We train to stay safe. We train to learn how to protect ourselves and those we care about.

Some people would like to buy their self-protection on line. Use some App and buy it using your Phone. This way they never need to venture out of their comfort zone.

When I began my training I ventured far away from my comfort zone. I was living in Brooklyn and there were plenty of locals teaching martial arts. There was even a "Jewish martial arts club", but I chose to go to a traditional Japanese school, but not just any school.

Even among the Japanese the Kyokushin style was known as the tough style, a black belt in this style was highly valued. Contact was hard and real.

I chose this style because I knew I had to leave my comfort zone. I wanted a place that would challenge me; I wanted a place where no one would go easy on me. So I left my comfort zone, the Jewish neighborhood, and I trained with Asians, Hispanics, Blacks and street kids. My world expanded. I would not trade that experience for anything.

As a teacher I see many students out of their comfort zone. I can see their anxiety but also their courage. Some are older, some are very short, some are office workers who have never trained in any contact sport or martial art.

They are all way out of their comfort zone.

The price for training is you venture out of your safe zone, you expose yourself to the fear of not doing well, to ridicule from your friends and family, to fear of failure and shame. You might get a little sore, a little banged up here and there, an accidental punch to the nose.

After three months in the Oyama dojo I made my first visit to the emergency room. I held no grudge against the green belt who gave me a roundhouse kick to the nose. Now I knew what it meant to see stars.

More visits would follow; broken hand, teeth, stitches; really no major injuries and nothing to complain about, just the bumps and bruises that come along the way.

We do our very best to avoid unnecessary injuries or pain. But this is maga, contact, and in every contact sport or activity there will be an occasional bump or bruise.

The price you pay for learning to defend yourself is like the price you pay for the flu shot; there will some minor pain, there will be some possible swelling and itchiness but in the long run it will be to your great benefit.

With Krav Maga you will have to leave your house and your comfort zone. You will meet some people who will initially scare you. Perhaps you will see some tough guys, police and military types or body builders. You will be leaving your comfort zone. The first shot to the nose may be a little uncomfortable but please remember…to achieve anything in life you must leave your comfort zone.

And I still remember, Brooklyn, getting up at 5 in the morning, leaving my comfy warm bed, going out in the snow, taking the train to New York City, seeing the Japanese Uchi Deshi, and starting some great training.

And it has all paid off.

To those about to train…we salute you.

# Feeling Proud
## October 30, 2015, New York, USA

Krav Maga Tour

Having just completed the Fall 2015 USA-Puerto Rico IKI Krav Maga tour I have reason to be proud. I am proud of our students and instructors.

This tour I have seen a new level among our instructors, a real improvement in the techniques and a deeper understanding of our IKI concepts. There is more of a flow, more of an ease.

But I have seen more.

I have seen a growing camaraderie among our IKI schools and instructors, not competition but cooperation. I have seen instructors from one school attending and supporting seminars of other schools. Each school is trying to help the other.

But I have seen more.

I have seen that our IKI instructors and students are standing up for what is right and good.

When I first started IKI I was "advised" to stick to martial arts. But IKI has never been only martial arts, nor has it only been physical self-defense. It has been about rising up, going the distance and standing up for what is right; To stand up and not back down.

To stand up to bullying, to stand up to emotional and physical abuse, to stand up to nonsensical political correctness, to stand up to terrorism, to stand up and fight the good fight for all that is right.

In Israel our students have responded to the recent surge in racist attacks against Jews and tourists by opening new classes and teaching all who wish to train, women, children, university students, older people. Our students have responded to the call, stood up and taken action. All of them have families, very full schedules, I do not know how they found the "free" time to do this, but ...they have.

All over the world our students are standing up to violence and racism. The names are too many to mention but....in Florida Joe Cayer is now reaching his 25,000th female participant in self-defense seminars. John Liptak and Gary Brielmayer are empowering young and old, men and women. For those who think "it cannot be done" just visit their class and you will see older guys training on a regular basis. You will find a 4 foot 9 woman fighting back. You will find people on the road to personal empowerment.

In Gulf Breeze Carrie and Scott are teaching women who endured years of abuse. In Colorado Todd just opened a huge facility where he teaches over 200 students. His staff, Kessany, Victor, Ashley and Brad helps him handle the needs of a diverse population, adults and children, military and civilian. In Georgia, Hal, in the 8th decade of his life is a living example of what can be done at any age. Teenagers, military and law enforcement and entire families come to train with him.

In Springfield Amy Jo is raising a generation of kids who know the meaning of respect and power. In Puerto Rico Jorge is already a legend among instructors. In Windsor Colorado Michael opened a class in a country barn and over thirty newcomers came to experience how one can defend and fight back.

Our instructors are standing up for what is right. They are taking up causes that matter. They are role models and guides.

Our IKI instructors are first and foremost ladies and gentlemen. We treat our students with respect and courtesy.

# See the Future
### Florida - New York, October 2015

Dedicated to the memory of Mr. Chaim Bieber

Back in December we released a new DVD, it was called "Defeat Hamas". The idea was to counter what our enemies were planning. The idea was to prevent the attacks that surely would come.

Hamas had just released a free video helping people learn how to kill Jews. Of course they wish to kill any infidels as well, which includes a large percentage of the world. We saw their video and together with videos taken from Israeli police surveillance cameras we studied their tactics and techniques and came up with realistic solutions to these problems.

We released this as "Defeat Hamas; Knife, Ax, Gun defense solutions". We sold a few hundred copies world-wide but not even five in Israel. Sad.

At one of our recent seminars in Florida, a student, Mark D. made a very astute observation. I mentioned that now in Israel we have been going through a turbulent period with an increase in individual attacks. These attacks are not major operations but individual attacks with simple weapons and directed against Israeli civilians. Mark pointed out that way back in December, as soon as we had the first sign of things to come, IKI released this DVD. We also posted blogs and encouraged people to train.

There was no response. Our classes in Israel did not grow and there was the usual lack of interest. Now with the recent attacks, suddenly, everyone is seeking Krav Maga instructors. Sadly there is a dearth of truly qualified Krav Maga instructors and all sorts of semi trained individuals with out of date skills are hosting classes and seminars. They are mostly teaching poor techniques that will not help anyone. This truly saddens me.

Mark pointed out that we had ample warning and that IKI was there with an immediate response, but no takers, and little to no interest. And now there are simply not enough qualified instructors to answer the need.

What I know to be equally true is that as soon as the violence subsides, which it surely will without any doubt, the interest in Krav Maga classes will also subside and very few students will remain. This is the sad truth I have learned in over thirty years of teaching in Israel.

Very few students will stay with us long enough to really develop skills.

Marks' wise words triggered some thoughts.

**Seeing the Future**

Back in 1897 a man named Dr. Theodor Herzl, also known by his Jewish name Binyamin Ze'ev Herzl held a conference. He had gathered leading Jewish figures from all over Europe for the First Zionist Conference. It was held in Basel, Switzerland, the date was August 29, 1897.

There are those that make things happen, there are those that watch things happen and there are those that do not know what happened. The great ones are in the first category. The mass of ignorant humans are in the last category.

That night a tired Dr. Herzl went home and made an entry in his personal journal. "Tonight I have created the Jewish state, it shall come to rise, it will be a reality in fifty years". He wrote a book called **Der Judenstaat** - The Jewish State. "Versuch einer modern Lösung der Judenfrage", (attempt, or proposal, for a modern solution to the Jewish question).

On the 14th of May, 1948 the third Jewish commonwealth, the modern state of Israel, came into existence. It was fifty one years after Herzl's prophetic diary entry.

There are those that make things happen.

"The Jews who wish for a State will have it."

A young Ze'ev, Vladimir, Jabotinsky, soon to become the father of modern Jewish militarism, was a disciple of Dr. Max Nordau. (July 29, 1849 - January 23, 1923).

Nordau himself had left Judaism to fully assimilate into German culture. Like Herzl the Dreyfus affair work him up from his delusion and brought him back to the Jewish fold. He became a Zionist.

Nordau raised the concept of what he called the "Muscle Jew", muskel-Judenthum. He understood there was a need for a change, to return to the old ways, the ways of the Biblical Jewish warrior.

19th century Zionist philosopher, Max Nordau, was quoted as telling Jewish leader Ze'ev Jabotinsky that "the Jew learns not by way of reason, but from catastrophes. He won't buy an umbrella merely because he sees clouds in the sky. He waits until he is drenched and catches pneumonia."

The late Rabbi Meir Kahane learned this lesson from Jabotinsky and told us many years ago... a man walks out of his house and sees clouds...but does nothing. He feels a drop of rain but does nothing. Catches pneumonia and runs to get his umbrella, this is the story of the state of the Jew during the period of the exile. (i.e. post the destruction of the Holy Temple of Jerusalem).

On so many counts, Nordau's words remain completely accurate and reliable today.

As Mark pointed out, back in December the Hamas publicly released their video on how to kill Jews and others. We took note.

Today suddenly people want classes after weeks of stabbings of innocent unprepared people. And the words of Max Nordau, from so many years ago, still ring true.

Will people ever learn?

This blog was inspired by Mark Dragonette's comment and is dedicated to the memory of Chaim Bieber, a dear friend who devoted his life to fighting for Jews.

Chaim was born in Brooklyn, NY, volunteered in the Israeli war of Independence for the establishment of the modern state of Israel. He was among the leading members of the Jewish Defense League for the protection of Jews in the United States, and his entire life was devoted to Judaism and his people. He passed away during this Krav Maga Tour. He merited to be buried in the State of Israel.

I will miss sitting across from him at the Shabbat table. I will miss the twinkle in his eye, and I will miss his gentle affectionate kiss on the cheek.

He was a true fighter and a man who always stood up for what he believed in.

He will be missed by all who knew him.

He was a warrior for Israel.

# The Gentle Way

NOVEMBER 1, 2015, NEW YORK

*Conclusion of Krav Maga Tour Fall 2015*

*With John Liptak and his wonderful group of instructors and students.*

When we think of great leaders, when we look back at history with the perspective of time, we see that the great ones were gentle. It is said that Moshe/Moses was the humblest of all men, that he was soft spoken. We are admonished to be "slow to anger and quick to forgive".

Leaders who rant and rave, shout and abuse, are remembered poorly. Hitler, Stalin, Mussolini, Muamar el-Gadhafi, Nasser, Saddam Hussein...

The "great" dictators had no regard for the lives of their own people. St Petersburg was said to be built on the bones of the Russian people.

And yet, sadly, in the Krav Maga and martial arts world all too often a soft and gentle approach is regarded as weakness.

Too many instructors feel they must bully their students, push them around a little, be tough. To me this is the truest sign of weakness and insecurity. They are more concerned with their own ego and image than with the needs of their students. IKI fights against this image which I believe scares away people who truly need our help and guidance

With an entire industry promoting the image of the Tough guy/Bad Ass Krav Maga instructor it is difficult to be *the man against the stream*. My true friends have always encouraged me to remain true to myself, to "keep doing what I am doing".

And so I have. Let people think what they think.

But the results speak for themselves.

I have stood in front of groups that included men twice my size, undercover police officers, prison guards, presidential guards, security experts, 5th *dan* black belts and 10th *dan* black belts, world champions and war heroes, and they have seen the essence of what matters. They have seen through the hype. They have understood that a gentle approach is a sign of confidence, not of weakness.

I do not need to hurt students to prove that it works. The stronger a person is, the more experience one has, the less effort it takes to prove the effectiveness of our methods. I do not need to have an open account with the nearest hospital.

But sometimes the greatest reward is when a smaller person takes the time to express how he or she felt when they came in, their fears and expectations, anxieties and doubts. And then to express how our approach works to alleviate those fears and create a true learning environment.

Below is a testimonial from one of our students. The woman stands about 4 foot 9, she is a student of IKI instructor John Liptak, a man who has proven himself in every martial arts context and combat and yet remains a quiet humble and gentle man. I am Very proud of him and the job that he does.

*I am a Krav student in Florida under John Liptak. My husband is Shawn Hill. I met you once last testing cycle and was inspired by all that you shared at your visit. I also read your book recently and really appreciated the opportunity to get to know more about Israel through your experiences. I look forward to meeting again next week.*

*I forgot that I had written some about my Krav experience a few months ago. I want you to know how much your hard work means to me . . .*

*Thank you for your dedication,*

*Jeannie Hill*

**My Krav Journey**

I started taking Taekwondo four years ago. I enjoyed the forms, but I hated the self-defense segments. Instead of feeling more confident, I left feeling vulnerable. The techniques were hard. They usually didn't work for my small stature. I couldn't find the pressure points and was unable to successfully complete the tasks. I laughed through these, masking a growing realization that I could not protect myself. I left training these days feeling insecure.

I started Krav at the begging of my husband. He loves it and would come home from class eager to show me what he had learned. After a friend's house was broken into, I decided that I might need more self-protection skills. Social media is full of images of thugs attacking the weak. The notion of "pick on someone your own size" seems to be a distant memory of a time when standards were somewhat intact.

I entered the door of John Liptak's Krav Maga training center and was slightly uncomfortable. Replicas of large guns lined the wall. The class was full of mainly men. I was thankful that my husband was able to show me around. Then John entered the room. His light-hearted and jovial personality put me at ease. He minimized the seriousness of the content with fun-loving banter. I was amazed at the simplicity of most of the moves. Even more amazing was the realization that it could be accomplished even by little old me. When the techniques didn't fit my size, John and the other instructors showed me specifically what I could do. Instead of feeling frustrated with what didn't work, I felt empowered by their ability to show me what would work.

I still struggle in class at times. The content is severe. For a man, the main thought is "who will win the fight". The worst the happens is death. If death were the only fear, it wouldn't be that bad. For a woman, the fear is capture. The fear is being locked in a basement and raped repeatedly. The fear is becoming a victim of human trafficking. There are times when we practice scenarios in class that cause these fears to surface. They bring the reality of my vulnerability in the open. I have never been attacked, but I still have the fear inside. The soothing and inspiring force that breaks through the fear is my instructors and the simplicity of Krav. *I used to leave each week wondering how they found this perfect balance...*

Meeting Moshe provided my answer. His gentle spirit entwined with his deep drive to help others embodies the spirit of Krav. The nation of Israel is like a victimized woman. They know the fear. They feel the pain of the past. They have haunting memories. From this, Moshi constantly works to help all.

I am past forty. I am under five feet tall. I have a plate in my back. I learn slowly. I bruise easily. After a year of Krav, my view of these issues has changed. The are no longer valid excuses. The simplicity and natural movements in Krav make it work for everyone. My insecurities are fading away as the techniques become more automatic. I will never be completely safe from harm, but I now know that I am far from defenseless...

# Krav Maga - Build On Weakness

###### November 4, 2015

Delta airline, US Fall Tour

We spend a good deal of our lives trying to hide our weaknesses. Entire industries are built on this idea. The whole makeup industry, (or whatever it is called, all the stuff people put on) is designed to cover up our natural flaws, our imperfections and signs of aging.

In other, older, societies, those "flaws" are signs of individuality, and "imperfections" that develop over time are signs of the life we have lived and the experiences we have gained, both good and bad. Our scars, our wear and tear, are part of who we have grown to become.

But in modern society we try to cover up everything. Whatever is seen as a sign of imperfection or weakness is covered up and hidden.

I love reading the Torah, the Bible. The stories never grow old. Nothing is hidden and nothing is covered up. Family feuds, jealousy, sexual desire, rivalries...it is all there. Even the greatest of men are presented with their weaknesses, David, Samson, Jacob, all great men, all had weaknesses, and the Bible records them for all eternity. It is for us to learn.

We too are imperfect, all of us. For no man has ever been created perfect and as the Bible says there is no man who shall never do wrong. We all make mistakes, we all have weaknesses, and there are no exceptions.

"כִּי אָדָם אֵין צַדִּיק בָּאָרֶץ, אֲשֶׁר יַעֲשֶׂה טּוֹב וְלֹא יֶחֱטָא"

As it says in Ecclesiastics, there is no man so righteous that he will always do good and never transgress.

We all have weakness.

I see the modern world of advertising as an attempt to cover up, to hide our weakness, and it occurred to me that IKI Krav Maga is the exact opposite. We are here to expose our weakness because only by seeing the truth can we build truthfully. We build upon an honest foundation, not upon illusions.

How so?

Imagine a teacher asks about the level of English in a class. Everyone says they are level 4. So the teacher begins with level 5. But in fact they are all level 2, beginners. So the teacher is building on a false premise and the students do not have the foundation to understand level 5. Better to be truthful and start where you truly are.

When I registered for college I asked to receive no credit for any other college courses I had taken. I said - Assume I know nothing, start me at the beginning. I want to learn the basics, the foundations.

With Krav Maga if I assume a certain speed, power of learning quickly, strength, ability to see the future and anticipate the attacks, well, I am basically creating a movie character, not a real person. Building upon what we wish we had rather than on what we actually have can only lead to disaster should a real situation actually arise.

The truth is a bitter pill. The mirror can scare us.

An athlete trains to be at his best. He will only compete when he is ready. He builds on his strengths. He will retire when he is no longer at his peak. With IKI Krav Maga we build on our weaknesses, and we train for life.

We assume that an attack will be difficult to predict, we will be caught by surprise to some extent. We assume this vulnerability and train accordingly. We do not train as if we know what is coming but we use the surprise to our advantage. We do not train to be supermen. We assume we will be afraid, caught off guard; we may have some physical limitations. We take all those into account with our training.

Building on our weakness means training realistically. We do what we can do based on our abilities. We certainly train to improve our abilities but we never lose track of what we can actually do. If kicking to the head or flipping a person in the air are not realistic possibilities for you, we shall not attempt it. We shall focus on what you can do, we keep it simple and effective and within the realistic range of your abilities.

We begin by exposing our weakness; physical, mental and emotional. We recognize our physical shortcomings, we recognize our limited ability to absorb new and complex techniques, we recognize our trauma and fear. Our style is based on all these weaknesses.

Hiding our weakness is counterproductive. Exposing our weakness is our true strength. We begin from weakness and develop it into our strength.

# Do Not Turn Back
### November 6, 2015, Israel

Finding the right spouse is never easy. Going back three thousand six hundred years our ancestor Abraham was seeking a wife for his son Isaac. He sent his trusted servant Eliezer on a mission...*Return to my homeland, my place of birth and take a wife for my son, for Isaac.*

But Eliezer had his doubts. Just as many of our exiled Jews are still reluctant to make the move to come to Israel, Eliezer was concerned that the woman he chooses might refuse to make the journey to the land.

Years earlier Abraham had been instructed by God to leave all he had behind and have faith and come to the Promised Land, the land of Israel. He accepted the command and made the journey, never knowing what the future would hold. Even today many of our people are not up to that challenge, and that is exactly what worried Eliezer.

He asked Abraham, *what if the woman does not want to come with me, should I return your son to the land from which you came?*

Abraham was emphatic. No!! Never. *"Beware, guard yourself against any such action lest you return my son to there."* (Genesis, 23, 6)

Abraham spoke of the great promise that God had made to him, of the great future, the future of the Jewish nation. This greatness would only come about in the

Promised Land, the Holy Land, the land of Israel. No, there can be no turning back!!

Eliezer was only the servant but Abraham was the master. While Eliezer was concerned about the woman's rejection of this Great Plan Abraham was not.

*God has made me a promise and it will be. God will send his messenger before you and you will take a wife for my son.*

Let us see the difference and let us learn.

Abraham could see the future, what we call today the big picture. Eliezer was worried; what if this goes wrong, what if that goes wrong. Great men move forward, no matter what. Obstacles are things to be overcome.

Abraham was a visionary; he could see what lesser men could not see. He was the man of God and the warrior. He would not turn back on his dream.

What if there is a challenge, what if the girl will not come along, should we turn back? Go back to whence I came from? Are you serious? A little obstacle and we turn back on our dream! No, Guard yourself from such thoughts, says Abraham. Guard yourself is the phrase he uses. Do not even allow these thoughts to enter your head.

You start a business, things *will* go wrong, oh yes indeed they will! So at the first sign of trouble close up shop and go back to your job which you hated?

You start training, someone makes fun of you, progress slows down; so you turn back on your dream! Think of

Abraham, there is no turning back, there is a great future ahead. If the girl says no, you are absolved from your oath. Forget about it, but never, never shall we turn back. We are on a mission; we have a goal.

As I read the words of our ancestor Abraham I feel the absolute determination in his soft voice. Words are used in command form; directions are clear and not subject to interpretation. You shall *not* return my son to that land. *This* is our land.

There is no turning back on a dream. Problems and difficulties shall arise and we shall deal with them. Objections will come from lesser men, we shall override them. But the dream must be a pure and holy one. Abraham does not say...If you fail I shall kill you, as a dictator would. No, if the woman does not want to come, so be it, we shall not force her, and you are exempt from any punishment and are absolved of our oath.

A strong will for a pure cause. Follow your dreams.

# Intelligence and Faith
### November 7, 2015, Israel

Intelligence and faith. We all seem to use both, at the same time.

I am speaking of blind faith that "everything will turn out fine". I am speaking of faith without reason.

In one aspect of our lives we are totally logical, of sound mind. While in other aspects of our lives we just hand matters over to "faith".

Albert Speer speaks of how he and other intelligent Germans were carried away by nationalist fervor, by the magnetism of Adolph Hitler. They followed him on faith and with total faith they believed they could win an unwinnable war. Any child could see that Germany had no chance.

Towards the end they knew the war was lost, but yet they still somehow had faith in Hitler.

On one hand they believed in Hitler and victory, on the other hand they knew the war was lost.

*"The latter step was an act of intelligence, the former of pure faith. The complete separation between the two revealed that special kind of derangement with which everyone in Hitler's immediate entourage regarded the inevitable end."* (Speer, 358)

In a sense we are all like this. We plan our finances. We have a pension plan, a medical plan, but do we have a self-defense plan? Do we have a home invasion defense plan? Do we have a plan for family defense in a crowded market place?

Or do we rely on faith in those areas of life?

As Speer says...complete separation.

Faith that everything will be OK: The writing was on the wall before World War Two. All the intelligence reports pointed to one clear conclusion. But the free world chose to act on faith, faith that "all would be OK". The price for this "faith" was more than sixty million dead people and a destroyed Europe.

What a bitter cold winter we prepare for ourselves. Hunger and starvation are for those who place their faith in idols.

Why do we use intelligence in some aspects of our lives while total, misplaced, faith in other aspects?

Is it because we are afraid to apply our intelligence to some areas as we are afraid of the conclusions? Why? Because the logical intelligence conclusions will dictate a response that we do not want.

Do we want to go to war? Do we want to devote two nights a week to Krav Maga training? Do we really want to look at our home and devote the time and expense to proper home security?

We do not, so we employ faith and not intelligence. We chose when to use our intelligence and when we prefer to leave it to faith. Faith means we are exempt from making an effort.

To clarify; I am speaking of a lazy faith, the belief, or the statement that "Everything will be OK". For true faith in a great ideal will actually entail *more* effort, more work. Those who fought for the establishment and freedom of the United States of America were not looking for an easy way out. They suffered bitter cold and deprivation, frost bite and hunger, but they had faith in their dream, so they endured.

However ignoring a problem and having "faith" that ...it will work itself out, is just the lazy man's way of saying that *someone else will have to deal with it and I sure hope they do because I will not lift a finger.*

As Albert Speer realized, way too late from the confines of his cell in Spandau prison (Berlin), people make a complete separation between areas where they employ faith and areas where they employ intelligence. He made this observation while serving a twenty year sentence for crimes against humanity. He made this statement after more than sixty million had died of a result of this faith. He was too late.

The question is will we be too late as well?

# Benefit of Doubt

NOVEMBER 14, 2014, MAALEH ADUMIM, ISRAEL

There are certain lessons we learn as children. Or rather I should say we are taught as children, but then we forget them, until someone reminds us.

I remember them well as my mother is a great teacher; there is a difference between retired and retarded, there is a difference between don't and doesn't, say, "My friend and *I* went to the store", not, "My friend and *me* went to the store".

Yes, I remember.

And there were other lessons;

Say your prayers before you go to sleep.

If you have nothing nice to say, say nothing.

Do not judge another until you stand in his place.

Give others the benefit of the doubt.

Yes, give others the benefit of the doubt. Damn that is a tough one!!

We see someone doing something "wrong" and we have this huge urge to rebuke them, here and NOW.

Later on it will turn out that we totally misunderstood the situation. Whoops! We made a huge error, we totally misjudged the person, but we have already publicly rebuked them. Oh well...

Last year we had a new student. He did not have a Krav Maga background; He was a Kung Fu expert, had been to China, and was clearly highly skilled.

And now he was trying out Krav Maga.

He was a quiet fellow, not very expressive.

I watched him during the training. He trained hard but did not say much. Some students let you know how they feel, but others are quiet.

And then I noticed something else, a little off. This Kung Fu guy seemed to be doing his Kung Fu forms and exercises. He would go off on the side and do his forms, (kata, or martial arts forms, *kanto* in Chinese).

He came to learn Krav so why is he doing Kung?

Let it be. No need to make a fuss. He does his own stretching, his own routines, he knows what is good for him. He is not a beginner. No need to make him "toe the line".

It is written in Proverbs, *"Teach the youth according to his own way. Even as he ages he shall not depart from the Way"*.

Teach him according to his way, not according to your way. No need to beat your students into submission, you are here to guide them, not dominate them.

I said nothing but wondered why he was doing his Kung Fu over here.

Weeks later I found out.

I overheard some of my students talking, *"That guy who was here for Tour and Train, did you see what he did? He took Moshe's Krav Maga techniques and he made them into a Kata, that is how he learns, that is how he remembers techniques".*

Wow. That was *his* way of remembering techniques.

In fact, he had paid me the highest compliment. This master martial artist had taken my techniques and elevated them to the realm of traditional martial arts forms. He had placed me along with the Chinese masters. A teacher can ask for no more.

Here I had thought that he was doing his own thing instead of trying to learn my techniques, thank God my mother taught me to give the benefit of the doubt and keep my mouth shut.

Today he is an IKI Krav Maga instructor and I am very proud of him. And I have been reminded of a very valuable lesson; always give the benefit of the doubt, even in your own mind! Never assume you know what is truly going on with another person. Learn to let go, learn to forgive, learn to give the benefit of the doubt. The results will please you.

Over time I have come to know this person, a man of true virtue and character, integrity and honesty, old school, real values.

*"Do not forget the lessons of your mother"* (Book of Proverbs)

*וְאַל תִּטֹּשׁ תּוֹרַת אִמֶּךָ*

# Quick to Judge

FRIDAY, NOVEMBER 13, 2015

As children, and as adults, we are constantly reminded not to be quick to judge others. Be careful how you judge others lest you be judged yourself.

Do not judge others until you have stood in their shoes, and does one man truly even live in another man's shoes?

You must walk a mile in another man's shoes to begin to understand him.

And yet we judge...

More often than not we find out later that we made a huge mistake. There were factors that we were not aware of, that we could not be aware of. I am currently reading a book about a son seeking forgiveness from his father. The son is Israeli, the father Polish-Jewish. The son was angry at the father and even encouraged his mother to divorce his father.

The father was an angry man and sometimes out of control. The son never understood his father, until it was too late.

After the death of the father the son heard an interview with the father, in the Polish language. He did not understand Polish as he did not want to learn the language of his father.

When he was told the content of the interview it sent him on a long search. He soon discovered that not only was his father a real hero but his father had saved his mothers' life during the war. That is why the mother would never leave her husband.

The father had seen death and suffering, torture and betrayal. He was a tormented soul.

How quick we are to judge.

The son had no clue what ghosts were in his father's soul.

Again and again I am stunned and shocked by those who are quick to judge. They see a little, hear what they want, use their own limited understanding, and pass judgment.

Even if we could read another man's mind we still would not be able to judge.

A story is told of a man who begged the holy rabbis to give him the power to read minds. The request was granted. He said Mr. Cohen is bad, but Mr. Gold is good.

Why? Mr. Cohen's mind was filled with young girls while Mr. Gold's mind was filled with holy books, the Bible, the Talmud. Surely the man with the power to read minds now knew who was good and who was bad.

But he was wrong, he was dead wrong.

Mr. Cohen was worried about young single girls. He wanted to find them suitable husbands. All day he thought about "his" little girls, would Rachel be a good match for Solomon, would Sarah be a good match for Jacob?

His mind was pure and holy. But Mr. Gold was a compulsive gambler and was in debt. His profession was book binding. So he thought of the holy books that perhaps needed binding. For a good binding of a Bible he could get $50, for a binding of a prayer book he can get another $30. He was all about the money.

Even a mind-reader can be wrong. God teaches us be slow to anger and quick to forgive and….to be careful before you judge others, most likely you will wrong.

# Pride and Fall

NOVEMBER 15, 2015, ISRAEL

All men shall die.

All who have been born shall also face death. Ashes to Ashes, dust to dust. From the first man it was decreed that all shall die. We are mortal. No man can escape the inevitable.

And yet we do not believe it. When death strikes we are caught by surprise. And equally true all shall be defeated at some point or another. No one remains champion forever. No one will leave this world with a perfect record.

Over 3,500 years ago the wise men of the Bible wrote that God humbles the mighty. *Pride precedes a fall.* It is the nature of life. As we grow older our bodies will deteriorate and fail us, and eventually we shall die. It is not my opinion, it is fact.

And yet we live with the arrogance of an undefeated champ. If one lives a life of humility than defeat is not an issue, it is a given. It is already taken into account.

If you run your business with the understanding that some months you will lose money than those months are not "defeats", they are part of a business cycle. It is part of nature. You build it into your system that some months will involve a loss.

Our style of Krav Maga is built on the premise, on the given that some people will be stronger than you. Some people will be able to defeat you in a fair competition. We build our techniques on the concept that you will be caught by surprise and overwhelmed. That truth is built into our system as a given. Thus "defeat" is not a humiliation; it is a factor we have already included.

There is nothing new under the sun. Goliath was defeated by David, Muhammad Ali was defeated. Every great champion was defeated. So it is wiser to accept this truth and live a humble life rather than shooting your mouth off. It makes it easier when defeat comes. And if you live the right kind of life, defeat is already integrated as part of your life. It is not defeat; it is merely part of your learning curve.

There is nothing new under the sun. The old wisdom stands the test of time. Arrogance is always ugly; humility and wisdom are always in fashion and look good at any age.

Better to become humble on your own rather than wait for it to delivered to you by the pounding fists of another.

True strength lies in wisdom.

# When Children Play
### November 16, 2015, Israel

I have just seen a very disturbing video. It shows Arab children in Israel playing as terrorists and Jews. Four children are waking down the street, they are all Arab children dressed as Israeli Jews. Three are wearing *Kipot*, the traditional male Jewish cap, while the fourth is wearing an Israeli army hat.

Another Arab child runs out of hiding place and quickly and efficiently stabs all four "Jews" while another Arab child is filming the heroic event. So all four "Jews" are on the floor reeling in pain, dying.

This is actually not so different from what goes on at many American university campuses. It is called "Israel Apartheid week"; Mock Israeli check-points are set up with students dressed as Israeli soldiers and other students dressed as Arabs. The "Israeli soldiers" check the Arabs by totally abusing them and degrading them. The implication is that Israeli soldiers are oppressing poor innocent Arabs.

This disturbing American phenomenon encourages hatred of Israel and Jews and promotes violence, and yet it is tolerated and encouraged on campuses the length and breadth of the United States, a country that was founded on the principles of the Jewish Bible. How things have changed. It is so sad that there is little difference between the Arab children's games and American university campuses. Both indoctrinate towards hatred.

In fact those check-points go out of their way to treat Arabs with respect. But let us first ask ourselves why these checkpoints exist. They exist because of Arab terrorism. They exist in order to stop Arabs from transporting terrorists and explosives and suicide bombers into Israeli cities.

When a bomb goes off it kills without discrimination. When a bomb goes off in the city center it kills Jews, Christians and Muslims. Yes, contrary to what the American college student believes we live together, we work together and we shop together. In every major bombing Muslims have also been victims. A bomb does not discriminate, we die together.

I drive by our local check point nearly every day; I have yet to see an Arab disrespected.

So Arab children play games simulating what their parents are doing, stabbing and killing Jews. This is a crime against their childhood by misguided parents, of this there is no doubt. Now my question is - What are our children doing?

I have been told to shut up and stop talking about the dangers of violence, lest innocent young ears hear my words and be frightened.

I have seen parents "protect" their children by refusing to expose them to violent programs such as the daily news. They do not want their children to grow up with fear. Instead their children grow up with illusions.

While other children are preparing for war our children are being molly-cuddled (molly cuddle - a pampered or effeminate man or boy). While other children are learning to attack, our children are watching Barney the friendly dinosaur.

In our neighborhood in Israel I have taught Krav Maga to children for two decades. These children grow up to be men and women who know how and why to fight.

Please take a moment to think about how you want to raise your children given the current state of the world. Just remember...other children are currently training to kill your children.

# Truth is Painful

NOVEMBER 24, 2015, ISRAEL

You would think that some things are obvious, that certain truths are self-evident; not in today's world.

In fact lies and deceit are as old as mankind.

Just as we learn self-defense to defend ourselves against knife attacks we also must learn self-defense to defend ourselves against lies and propaganda. We must begin this training very young or else we will never know the truth from a lie. Education matters.

When a Jewish child begins his education he starts with the Torah, the five books of Moses. He needs to know his history, he must know who he is and from whence he came. He must establish a strong identity. When he begins his study of the Talmud it is with the tractate of "The Middle Gate", *Bava Metzia* (in Aramaic).

*Come and study with me...*

CHAPTER I

MISHNAH

Two [persons appearing before a court] hold a garment one of them says, 'I found it', and the other says, 'I found it'; One of them says, 'It is all mine', and the other says, **'It is all mine',**

*"Two are holding on to a garment..."* The child learns that two are disputing the ownership of a garment. The rabbis explain that this is not directly related to the rest

of the discussion but it establishes important principles; ownership and truth.

Note that the item under discussion in the *Mishnah* is the *tallith*. At the time this was a large, rectangular piece of cloth with ritual fringes *(tzitzith)* worn as an outer garment by men (roughly analogous to the Roman toga). It survives in the present day as the *tallith koton* ("prayer shawl"). The tallith is used as an example here for three reasons. First, since the tallith **was** an outer garment, it common for men to remove it before doing physical labor (as with a coat or jacket in modern times).

Thus, it was not uncommon to find a lost *tallith*, blown away by the wind or simply forgotten by its owner. Second, whilst the *tallith* might be woven of stuffs of different textures and/or colors (although not, of course, of different materials), it was essentially just a piece of cloth. In chapter 2 of *Bava Metzia*, we learn that Torah law requires us to return a lost object to his owner, provided that it has such identifying features as to make us reasonably certain that the claimant is in fact the owner, and not someone seeking to claim it for his own gain. A *tallith* is quite likely to be lacking such identifying features, and thus may be justly claimed by the finder. Third, a *tallith*, being as mentioned before, essentially just a piece of cloth, is thus capable of being physically divided without destroying its value, as would be the case if the item under dispute were, e.g., a live donkey."

The young Jewish child learns that absolute truth does exist. The child learns that what belongs to another must be returned to its rightful owner. The concepts of truth and ownership become embedded in the child's mind. I can still recall learning these concepts myself back as a young boy in the Shilo elementary school in Kiryat Ono. Can you imagine the impact?

But not everyone was raised this way. Not every boy fell asleep after reciting the bed time prayers with his dear mother; the prayer proclaiming the unity of God and the people of Israel.

It seems that no matter how obvious something is, no matter how clear as day, it will still be subject to being twisted beyond recognition.

The Jews have been victims of such lies for millennium.

A few years ago a certain group spread lies about Jews, nearly the entire world bought it, hook line and sinker. A people that has contributed more than any other nation of similar size, been awarded more Nobel prizes, been recognized for more inventions, has been victimized beyond recognition. And most of the world buys it.

So we came home. And now in the Land of Israel, known as the State of Israel, it continues. An Arab woman comes with a knife, she comes to kill, she has every intention to kill. Yes, she may be a mother of three, she may be a doctoral student at the university but she is also a terrorist and today she came to kill.

But she was stopped. She was stopped because we have become very careful and alert. She was stopped by a police officer. He warned her to stop.

She did not listen.

He warned her in her own language.

She did not listen.

He shot in the air.

She did not listen.

So the police officer responded correctly. He shot her dead. She came with the intent to kill and the knowledge that she might face opposition. Her fate is her own doing.

It was all caught on film, every aspect of it. You would think that all would agree, but...there is a "Counter Argument", it goes like this. A sweet innocent woman, a wife and a mother of three, a doctoral student at the university, was on her way home when she was brutally murdered by the cruel Israeli "Occupation Forces" (Since they believe Jews have no right to be here, or anywhere).

After the "murder" the Israelis put a knife next to the "victims'" lifeless body. Of course the video is dismissed, that is the way of propaganda, ignore all truth long enough and people will agree with you.

The truth is painful. The truth might expose that your entire cause is a fake and a fraud, that in fact you have no case at all, no claim at all. I understand this is difficult to accept. I recall a story of a man, an old man who lived his entire life as a devoted Communist when finally at a ripe old age he came to understand that it was all a waste of time, a big lie that he bought into. He felt his life was wasted. But I disagree.

I admire that man. His life was not a waste because at the end of his life he became a shining beacon of truth. Without having lived eighty years with a mistaken ideology he would not have become the hero that he became, to see the truth, to admit the truth, after eighty years. That is powerful. That man is a hero.

Truth can be painful. But it must be faced; otherwise you live your life as a lie.

This is our policy with IKI Krav Maga, and this is why we are constantly improving our techniques. We have a technique, we like it, we believe in it but...we are always keeping our eyes open. Sometimes we see it is too difficult for most people to learn this technique. Sometimes we see it applied on the street and we notice there is need for change or improvement. Whatever the reason; everything is always under observation.

So IKI Krav Maga continues to live a life in pursuit of truth, on and off the training mat. Truth may be painful and inconvenient but there is no other way to live.

# Adapting Adjusting Defense

### December 2, Thailand

We must always be adapting. We must always be taking in new information and improving our situation. Unless we want to remain where we are and fall behind the rest of the world we must adapt and change.

Even the most primitive societies are constantly adapting and adjusting. It may appear to outsiders that no changes are taking place but yet a careful study will show that in fact great changes have taken place.

When we study "primitive" societies we discover that in order to survive they had made constant changes and improvements. Some of the inventions they have come up with are simply beyond words, phenomenal and ingenious. In the way they preserve water, collect food, stay warm and safe from the environment and enemies; constant adjustment and improvements, and so must we.

On Tour and Train, we visit Masada and students always ask; but how could they live up here? How did they gather food and water? The answers show that in many ways they found solutions far superior to what we have today. While our food is genetically modified to last a few weeks King Herod had organic food that was still fresh seventy years after he left it. And while today our top scientists are still struggling with the water issue King Herod, and later the Jewish rebels, never lacked for water, in the middle of a desert, on the top of a secluded mountain.

I am currently in Thailand, much is new and different. As always I try to prepare by reading about a culture, by speaking to those who have been here, but yet it is never enough. The basic principles of keeping your eyes open, watching your back and expecting the unexpected still applies.

While it is true that "people are people" there are still major cultural differences around the world and different cultural norms. Not knowing the local rules can get you in a lot of trouble.

While researching a culture is certainly helpful there are still some things one must learn on their own, and we try to learn them without a heavy cost. As we always stress…Self Defense/Krav Maga is much more than physical. We have a mind and we must use it.

You can train all day but without the correct mind training it will be of little use. Just imagine a plumbing problem; a man comes in with a bulldozer, a sledge hammer, a drill and just starts smashing things up. That is what dentistry used to be like, destroy the tooth and build a new one; Terrible waste. Taking the time to see the problem fully, to understand where the danger might come from, and the correct measured response, is far more useful than the number of push-ups you can do or how many punches you can throw per minute.

While walking around Bangkok last night with my friend and fellow IKI instructor Tyler Collins we observed people's behavior. I offered my thoughts while he added more useful information based on living here for nearly a year.

Watching people, how they interact, how they are dressed, even the depth of the tans...reveals so much. Self defense, survival, Krav Maga is a matter of constantly observing people, picking up detail, noticing the nuances.

While my observations were more general and superficial Tyler was able to offer more insight having spent more time in Thailand. Things are not always as they appear or as you read on the internet. Personal, hands on experience, is necessary. We must always be learning. We must be paying attention.

Our self-defense training is constantly evolving. It is not only physical, it is not only watching your back, it is also monitoring the political and social environment; it is being aware who might decide to hate you for reasons only they understand. Self-defense is following the political and social climate changes. In Thailand no one seems to know anything about Israel or Jews, thus wearing Jewish attire puts you in no trouble at all. Yet on many college campuses in the Western world today just wearing any sign of Jewishness or support for Israel will put you in grave danger. Even wearing our Krav Maga T shirts has been enough on occasion to "provoke" haters and racists into abusive and violent behavior.

Keep training, stay in shape, sharpen your mind, keep your eyes open and watch your back. Training never ends.

Watch your step, look both ways before crossing the street and... train in Krav Maga.

With IKI instructor, Black Belt, Tyler Collins.

# Age of Distraction
### December 3, 2015, Israel

We always stress that we must prepare for tomorrow's attack, not only yesterday's attacks. I recall when I first starting touring the USA and Canada and teaching Krav Maga on college campuses I was told that while gun defenses were "fun" they really had no practical purpose as guns were banned on college campuses.

I think there is no need to comment on that.

Similarly I was told by British and French guests that certain "Israeli problems" were not relevant for them and they would prefer I not waste their time with irrelevant training. They wanted to dictate their own curriculum.

Again, there is no longer a need to comment.

Similar situation with airport security, after someone brings a liquid bomb on board we can no longer bring our toothpaste in our hand-luggage, and yet when my dear friend Prof. Cohen approached them with a bag full of non-metallic weapons that could breach their security, none were interested.

Who is wise? He who sees the unborn. And who is foolish? Well, we already know.

Our local enemies started with rock throwing. Soon all Israeli vehicles paid extra for special protection and special windows. The problem went away. Then there were knife attacks, shooting, suicide bombings. As each problem was solved the enemy moved to another attack.

In recent times there was a sudden re-emergence of knife attacks. Tragically several Israelis were killed.

For years I had been like a prophet of old, pouring my heart out to the masses and urging people to train in Krav Maga. However contrary to the image propagated by other Krav Maga associations Israelis are not well trained in Krav Maga; not the civilians, not the police, and no, not even the military. Here we have known the truth for a long time.

The myth served commercial purposes quite well; every graduate of the Israeli army is an expert in Krav Maga and fit to start his/her own organization and hand out black belts. What a fool believes.

So the myth grows and unqualified Israeli "instructors" spring up around the world like mushrooms after a rain but it is all a lie. And soon the lie is exposed.

### *The truth emerges*

When the recent knife attacks emerged the truth became known; no one had a clue how to defend themselves. Even combat veterans and officers were easily stabbed and killed by Arab teenagers. The truth is there for anyone willing to see. The IDF does not produce Krav Maga experts. Thus I refuse to advertise "As taught by the IDF". No chance. Here we know the truth.

And now the knife attacks, while still continuing, are having different results. They no longer end in the deaths of Israelis or innocent Arabs, who have also been the victims of these attacks as we look similar, but now the deaths are of those who come to kill.

You see no one has suddenly emerged as Krav Maga experts but they have become more aware. And this has made all the difference.

Many Israelis carry weapons but until now were unsuccessful in pulling them out in time to stop an attack. Now, as if by magic, nearly all the knife attacks end in the attacker being shot dead on the spot.

What has changed?

What has changed is a fundamental human error has been corrected, an error that should not have happened in the first place, not here.

I have always stressed that the key to self-defense is awareness, not the size of your biceps or the number of push-ups you can do. We stress simple techniques coupled with constant awareness.

What is amazing here is that Israelis, who should know better, were living as if this was a club med resort. This is not acceptable!

Our survival, all of us, all over the world, depends first and foremost on awareness, constant awareness. Let our enemies know we will not be caught off guard. Let them also know we are training and will not be easy targets. Sadly the Israeli population of this generation has been found lacking. They needed a wakeup call; sadly it was a bloody wake up call.

This is the age of distraction. I watch people, I see ten people, nine of them are on their Dumb Phones; sitting ducks I tell you.

Awareness and effective Krav Maga training that is what we offer here.

There are two ways to learn, by failing or by observing others. Be smart.

# A Thousand Miles

### December 2015, Thailand - Israel

I noticed writing on the wall in Thailand, in English. Something along the lines of .... One thousand miles of travel is no longer than one mile when you travel for love.

I understand. When you are in love a journey of 1,000 miles or even longer nowadays, is no longer than one mile. You are so eager to see the person that the travel time and distance do not matter.

I get it, sort of...If we apply it to martial arts training.

No effort is too much for the things you really want. This truth is as old as time itself.

I imagine in ancient times no one ever said they had no time for hunting or harvesting. Well if they did they died out and their descendants are no longer among us. Such people do not survive as a race.

I imagine no nation ever said they had no time for forming self-defense groups. Every ancient nation had its warriors or else they did not survive. Those are what we call self-correcting problems.

If you do not plant, hunt, harvest, gather essential food in one way or another, you will perish. If you do not learn to defend yourself, as an individual or as a nation, you will perish.

And yet today we ignore this.

We destroy our natural resources, we ignore vital issues, and we plant the seeds of our own destruction.

Why? Because as powerful as is the desire to survive, greed and laziness are also very powerful. When greed and laziness win we all lose.

Over the years I have travelled more than a thousand miles for my training, much more. When I would attend Karate College it took a full month's salary to cover my trip and training, but I did it.

When I first joined the Oyama dojo Sensei Romero said to me, "Our students pay their dojo dues before they pay their rent". That is when I knew it was the right place for me.

When you make something a priority there is always time and money for it. When you travel for love a thousand miles is no longer than one mile. When you travel for martial arts training the same is true. Our students have travelled to Israel to train with us from all over the world. A thousand miles is as one. As Rabbi Wehl used to say, "It is all a matter of priorities".

# Lowest Common Denominator

December 5, 2015, Israel

Math is not everyone's favorite subject. In fact many fear math more than any other subject in school, however! However you cannot argue with the fact that math is logical. Math does not depend on your personal point of view, on your mood or your attitude. Math is fact and when you are wrong you simply cannot argue about it. (Well, you can but you will still be wrong and it can be proven).

At IKI Krav Maga we take the math approach to providing solutions. They must work and they must make sense. And, like math, they cannot discriminate; they must make equal sense for everyone, at all times.

But how can we prove it? How can we prove which methods are the most effective? Unlike math there is no simple formula and there are so many different variables, however we do use the mathematical concept of LCD, Lowest Common Denominator.

In Math, everything is reduced to the simplest possible terms, instead of 84/168 we simply use 1/2, much simpler. Instead of 252/168 we use 1.5, more user friendly. At IKI we reduce the techniques to their simplest components and work from there. A few simple concepts apply to a vast variety of situations.

But we use LCD in another way as well. We test our techniques by using the weakest, smallest person we can find. I just saw a video where some big guy was "defending" against his students who were choking him. The method he used worked great, for him, against his students who were not really making any major attempt to grip and crush his throat. But we know what would happen if it were a big strong muscular guy grabbing the throat of a petite woman - Not A Chance! Tried and tested, does not pass the test.

I constantly see photos of instructors grabbing the attackers' arm, my goodness!! How could they? The grab does not work, it defies logic, maybe if you are Arnold Schwarzenegger, but even then it will work only on film. At our seminars and class we show over and over again why the grab does not work under real life conditions. But yet....it is still being taught. Something is going wrong over here.

Anything, anything at all, can look good on video. Just watch the movies, it all looks great but it is Fake, Fake, Fake. Sadly, looking good is no indication whatsoever that a technique is effective or at all useful.

The public is being deceived, buyer beware.

The source of the problem is a lack of honesty. Too much goes untested. Our techniques are constantly being tested and re-evaluated; Whatever we are doing in Israel is taught all over the world, they can practice and then ask questions. Often these questions lead to new discoveries and improvements.

While big numbers look impressive they are not easy to work with. Lowest common denominator helps us reach effective solutions that are valid for all.

It must be simple.

It must be effective.

It must be user-friendly for all types of people under real-life conditions.

# Philosopher's Table
### DECEMBER 7, 2015, TEL AVIV

It is a philosophical time, the Festival of Lights, the holiday of Chanukah, or Hanukah, the victory of Judah the Maccabee and the Jewish rebels over the Greeks and the Hellenists, the struggle to preserve the Jewish way of life. We are the people of the book and the people of the Talmud; we discuss, debate and analyze.

My mother told me a story she heard from my grandfather. An outsider comes to town, he sees a large building and it is surrounded by "taxis" of that era, i.e. the horse and buggy, or in Hebrew/Yiddish the *Ogoloh,* עגלה.

He says to a local, "I assume there is a great convention going on inside, learned men who came to hear a lecture, I imagine. And the wagons belong to the taxi drivers who must have gone to the local pub for a drink until the event is over."

"No" responds the local. "These are Jewish drivers, *Ba'alei Ogolo*, wagon-men, cab drivers, and at the end of a long day of hard work driving all over the city they come here, to the *Beth Midrash*, the House of Study, to discuss the Talmud, the holy books. The drivers *are* the scholars."

The visitor was stunned. He assumed that the simple drivers were at the pub waiting while the intellectuals were in the House of Study. *"Ah...Who is like thy nation Israel, a unique nation on earth..."* (Samuel, book 2, chapter 7, 23)

Today at the T shirt factory I shared the same experience. While working we discussed the Jewish history of Łódź, Poland, and the development of Łódź as a force in the textile industry. Yisrael, one of the owners of the factory, comes from a family from Łódź, his forefathers were key players in the textile industry before the war.

We continued to discuss with Alon some Jewish genealogy and the effects of the in-gathering of the exiles back to Israel and the impact on our identity.

We discussed the miracle of Chanukah and the battles of the Maccabees.

And then Yisrael, with a cigarette in his hand and no yarmulke (head covering) on his head, begins expounding the weekly Biblical Torah portion.

When one of the workers was a little surprised Yisrael said to him, *"You should open the Torah, the Bible, and study. Every time I study it I uncover something new"*.

*"You study the Torah?"* asked the other worker.

*"Of course! Every week. And every Friday I listen to the lessons of Rabbi Elboim. So much to learn."*

I thought of my late father and how he would always say, *"Many who appear to be non-practicing Jews are in fact quite deeply Jewish, if you watch them closely."*

The factory owner expounding the Torah, discussing Jewish history, encouraging others to study, Ah...Who is like thy nation Israel, a unique people in the land...Even the empty ones among you are filled with Judaism like a pomegranate. (Talmud, Sanhedrin)

I left with an elated feeling. These T shirts are not ordinary T shirts, just as the wagon drivers were not simple wagon drivers. May the words of the Torah always be on our lips, may the wisdom of the rabbis never depart from our conversations, and may the ordinary always be elevated to the extraordinary.

# Faith

December 8, 2015, Israel

*"There is something inside that they cannot touch, hope" (Andy)*

*"Let me tell you something my friend - Hope is a dangerous thing. Hope can drive a man insane." (Red)*

Faith: A controversial topic. Are the faithful the enlightened ones or is "Religion the opium of the people." Is the age of enlightenment one where people finally throw off the primitive yoke of religion, or is enlightenment when people finally realize the truth that this universe is more than a series of random coincidences, that a divine force is guiding us, that we are never alone?

Is faith truth or an illusion? Who possess the truth, the believers or the atheists?

The debate began long ago and is far from having run its course.

But there is another question. Many will argue that faith gives hope. There is no doubt that those with religious faith have something to believe in, something to hope for, and this gives them peace. And yet the non-believers will argue that it is a false hope, a grand illusion, nothing but deception.

Some religions stress that faith will motivate one to take action; you believe and so you go out on a Holy Crusade, or Jihad. As part of your faith you either forcibly convert others, or just kill them. The more civilized will just drive you crazy, knocking down your doors and trying to convert you to the "true faith". They will preach eternal damnation for those who reject their particular savior.

And some faiths will preach lack of action; Accept, submit. The debate is; is hope a good thing or a bad? The movie The **Shawshank Redemption**, a true classic, tackles this issue honestly, is hope a positive factor in our lives, or a negative. Andy believes in hope, Red does not.

You might say Andy represents the religious idea that hope gives people reason to live, to go on despite the tragedies of life. Thus hope is a good thing. Red represents the idea of acceptance, i.e. hope is the source of pain, give up hope and accept life as it is: Zen. Once you accept your situation you can deal with it. Hope creates expectations, these will not be fulfilled and thus you will go crazy. It is better to just accept your situation.

Every kid in America grows up with the idea that he could be president, he could play in the major leagues. Of course only one person will be president every four years, and only a few hundred will play major league baseball.

At a certain point in life most of us accept that we will never be a major leaguer, we will not pitch in the World Series, and we will not be president of the United States of America.

Once we accept that we can move on to regular productive lives. Acceptance frees us from unnecessary pain.

And yet, for those who truly dream of the stars, hope is essential. Some child dreamed of walking on the moon, and it happened, someone dreamed of flying the air, and it happened, someone dreamed of a phone that did not need to be attached to the wall, and it happened. Someone now is dreaming of a cure for cancer, let's not crush his hope.

Hope is powerful.

Hope or no hope, Andy and Red, the debate continues.

And then I must ask, what kind of faith are we speaking of? Active or inactive. For there is a faith that is designed to spur to action, and there is a faith designed to keep us inactive, under control.

One of the legitimate claims against organized religion is that far too often throughout history it has been controlled by powerful men, powerful organizations that are inherently corrupt. That is why Adolf Hitler so admired the Church. He too wanted blind obedience, he so admired an organization that could keep people under control for 1,500 years and not question authority. Blind faith serves the purposes of our leaders. He studied the methods of the Church in an attempt to instil the same faith in his followers, faith in him as a leader.

For such reasons people of faith have been mocked.

And yet faith has motivated great fights for freedom. Today we celebrate Chanukah where Mattathias the High Priest of Israel rose up against the invaders and called out

"Whoever is for God join with me" and he and his sons proceeded to victory.

Faith can come in different forms.

People say "believe in yourself" but what does this mean? Are you making yourself a god and replacing God the creator? Who are you!

In fact what is being said, whether it is understood or not, is that your creator has given you incredible powers. Believe in those powers, believe you can achieve great things, for this is the reason you were created.

Believing in yourself is actually a great belief in God, for if you believe in the product than you believe in he who created this wonderful product.

But belief and faith can also lead to passivity. Many, both secular and religious, believe that all will be good and we need not bother to make an effort. The religious will say, "Trust in God, he will solve all the problems". The secular will say, "Do not worry; things have a way of working themselves out."

I believe both to be wrong.

Faith is not the sole possession of the "religious".

Faith should not be an excuse for not taking action. We all know..."God helps those who help themselves".

Faith is energy to make a difference, to get off the couch and believe you can move mountains. Faith is not an excuse for lack of action. Lets us not confuse faith for laziness.

I believe that faith is a force that will spur us on to take action, as long as it is still possible, and to accept that which we cannot change, once action is no longer possible.

When religious Jews walked into the gas chambers, knowing their fate but yet having exhausted all opportunities for resistance, they knew they were going to another life, another dimension, that the soul is eternal and that their death was an act of proclaiming their faith. For those with no faith it was just the end of the road, dust to dust.

While we live, while we have options for action, faith can be an active force in our lives. Whether you call it faith in God, faith in the Universe, the Force, or faith in yourself, it is still faith.

Keep the faith and it will keep you.

Krav Maga is an act of faith. It is the act of believing that by taking action you can indeed make a difference. Those who say, *why train? I will never be able to defend myself or overpower a larger opponent,* lack faith. They lack faith in themselves, they lack faith in their teachers. But most of all they lack faith in life.

Those who say, *I do not need Krav Maga, I have faith that God will protect me*, is, I believe, a false faith, the lazy man's way of saying I cannot be bothered.

Dream...before it is too late.

*"Get busy living or get busy dying" (Red, Morgan Freeman, The Shawshank Redemption)*

# Peace ~ Yehi Shalom

### December 9, 2015, Third day Chanukah, Kislev 27,

Let there be peace.

Let there be peace in your dwelling place, calm in your palaces

May there be peace within your ramparts, peace in your citadels.

**Yehi Shalom**, Let there be peace.

So sang great grandfather David, the sweet singer of Israel, and so we pray today.

But David was a warrior, and so must we be.

Today is Chanukah, the Festival of Lights, let there be light in the world, peace. But today is Chanukah where we celebrate how our forefathers, the Maccabees and the Jewish rebels, defeated our enemies. Peace can be achieved through war.

We pray for peace, we work for peace, but we must prepare for war.

Krav Maga is this idea in a personal form. There is the state, the military, the Special Forces, the police and then us; we are the first line of defense. We must take personal responsibility for our safety.

I cannot bear to hear more stories of knife attacks, I cannot bear to see more people crying, I cannot handle any more funerals. The pain is too great. But yet I know that our people have suffered much more than this, and survived. The Crusades, the massacres, the pogroms, the holocausts, ...but now we have the Third Jewish commonwealth and the Israeli Defense Forces.

Sweet singer of Israel, we use your ancient words and we pray for peace, but we lift up the sword of the Maccabees and we prepare for war. And the warriors of old are with us. To my right is Michael....

And Sweet singer Shlomo tells the story of a fourteen year old boy who was studying the holy Talmud, World War Two, and the evil ones came in, and killed his newborn baby brother, and laughed. *Al eila l bochiya*, for these I cry...

And we cried so much, oceans of tears, dark times when the gates were closed. A song can open a gate, a sword protects it. Be a Maccabee; hold on to your sword.

How can a baby be slaughtered and men in uniform are laughing? And the world learns nothing. For these I cry...and for these I fight.

The world is a place of great kindness and great evil. We pray for peace, we train for war.

We walk with our ancestors, we lift up their swords and continue the struggle, we use their words and their swords. The spirit is one. The spirit is alive.

We march forward. On this Chanukah day we light the candles, we kindle the spirit and we continue the struggle, as we pray for peace and continue our training.

In the name of the holy ones we continue, in the name of God, the God of Israel, to my right is Michael, to my left is Gabriel, in front of me is Uriel, and behind me is Rafael, and on my head is the presence of God.

We march forward but we are never alone.

בשם ה׳ אלוהי ישראל: מימיני מיכאל, משמאלי גבריאל,
מלפני אוריאל, מאחורי רפאל ועל ראשי שכינת אל

# Connection

DECEMBER 10, 2015, FOURTH CANDLE OF CHANUKAH, 28 KISLEV, ISRAEL

The Jewish people have suffered for a long time in many lands. We were kicked out of more countries than most school children can name. We were the victims of more ruthless rulers than any of you can spell. We were exiled from our land and forced to wander the world, *"The Wandering Jew"*. What a journey it has been.

We have been to hell and....Back!

That hell has many names; Auschwitz, Treblinka, Sobibor, Siberia, Spain, Italy, Frankfurt, Arabia, Iran, Iraq, Babi Yar....

Our tormentors wore many uniforms.

Along the way many lost their faith, many gave up. As in the Marines...many rang the bell and said, "I have had enough, I quit".

They gave up because as my grandparents said...*Shver a zijn a yid*, it is difficult to be a Jew. Or as Tuvia Beilski answered when his friend said, "Why is it so hard being the friend of a Jew", Bielski responded, "Try being one."

But it is not only difficult, it is also beautiful. So we hang on.

When I was younger I heard the following from a rabbi, something from hundreds of years ago. *A time will come, my friends, a difficult time will come, and many will lose their hope, many will lose their faith. It will be as two angels holding on to a rope, and the people are hanging from the rope for dear life. But as time goes on the angels will shake the rope harder and harder, faster and faster. It will be difficult to hold on to your faith, to your way. Many will give up and let go. I am telling this to you now so when the time comes you will know to hold on tight.*

Those words have remained with me always; they have become part of my life. Hang on! Do not let go, no matter how difficult it is, keep hanging on, for it is worth it.

Do not lose that connection. Do not let go. We all go through difficult times. In Israel we say, we survived Pharaoh we shall survive this. We can handle it.

Every day for the past 2,000 years we have spoken of the redemption of Zion and the return. Along the way we lost many, many lost hope, many lost their faith in the way of the nation of Israel. But those who stayed strong were rewarded, for after nearly two thousand years the remnant walked out of Auschwitz, they walked from Yemen, from Baghdad, from Siberia, from the Gulag and from the concentration camps and from the luxury of America, and they came home. My friends, it took a long time.

As a nation and as an individual, we must never lose hope. In fact "The Hope", HaTikva, is our national anthem. Remember, two angels will be shaking that rope, I am telling you so that you remember to hold on tight: Do not let go, do not allow yourself to fall into the abyss. Hang on.

Do not lose hope.

I recall something I heard many years ago from a Chasid, a follower of the Rebbe from Breslov, Ukraine. He said as long as you alive it means that God has not given up on you. So if God has not given up on you how can you give up on yourself? Remember, two angels will be holding a rope and shaking it hard, I am telling you so that you remember not to let go. For many will fall.

And I recall another story, from the holy Rabbi Yisroel Salanter. (November 3, 1810, Zhagory – February 2, 1883, Königsberg). As he was walking home late one night he saw the candle was still burning in the home of the local shoemaker. It was late at night and the poor "sandler" was still awake, fixing shoes. The rabbi walked in and said, *"Why are you up so late?"* The simple man responded, *"As long as the candle still burns there is still time to fix and mend, to repair".*

The rabbi immediately saw the spiritual connection and was ecstatic. He walked home and kept repeating like a mantra...*As long as the candle still burns there is time to fix and mend...*

In Judaism the candle is likened to the soul of man. The candle of God is the soul of man. (Proverbs, chapter 20). As long as we live there is still time to fix and to mend, it is never too late. A garment that is torn will never be new again, but a soul, a soul can always repair itself. As long as the candle yet burns....

Days are coming...when there will be hunger, but not for bread, nor thirst for water, but for the word of God, for the truth, stay strong as the angels shake that rope, for many will fall. Hang on tight.

The wait is worth it.

*There is no greater illness than discouragement! (Rabbi Yisroel Salanter)*

# Quitters and Winners
### December 11, 2015, Israel

During my travels around the USA I have often heard the phrase, "Quitters are not winners, and winners are not quitters". Well, that may not be entirely true.

Recently an undefeated female MMA champion was defeated, badly defeated. She was defeated in a way that could almost be called an embarrassment. What made it worse was she was so totally arrogant.

There is nothing wrong with losing a match, there is nothing wrong with losing a game. Have you ever seen a baseball team end the season 162-0? No, this does not happen, losing is part of the sport. We all lose sometimes and yet we do not lose our dignity.

But this woman had her mouth running like a female version of Muhammad Ali, ..I am the greatest, I am the best, there is no one like me.

It got to the point where she was saying, "What shouldn't I be proud of myself and my body?"

Well she certainly should be proud, but not arrogant. Pride precedes a fall.

There is a huge difference between pride and arrogance. No one stays on top for ever. While you are relaxing and enjoying your victory some kid in the slums is pounding the heavy bag and picturing your face on it. There is someone hungrier than you.

Humility and respect for others is always in style. You never put yourself down by being a little humble and showing proper respect for others. And if we ever do get a little feeling of...I am super great; just remember, no one stays on top for ever. And remember that in the end we all die and perish from this earth, we are not immortal or eternal.

The Talmud reminds us ...remember from where you came, a smelly drop, and where you will end up, dust.

This should keep us humble.

Now this particular woman, after losing her fight, came out with quite a statement. A rematch was arranged but she said that if she loses, that's it, she is quitting, hanging up her gloves.

I am not here to judge her. Everyone retires at some point, that is her personal choice and I am sure she has her reasons, none of my business.

My point here is the lesson for others; do we quit as soon as things do not go our way? Abraham Lincoln lost many elections but never gave up, he eventually changed America. The Beatles were turned down by numerous record companies but eventually changed the face of music. Bruce Lee was rejected for role after role but eventually opened the door for Asian actors and changed the way we look at martial arts.

These men are role models. These men inspire us.

These men did not quit, and they changed our lives for the better.

The lesson must be that yes, we will all encounter obstacles, temporary setbacks, but we do not announce that if the next episode does not go our way we are quitting. No.

I would say some winners are also quitters, but those who ultimately make a difference are those who do not fear defeat, those who never give up.

The Jewish nation lost their independence in the year 135. We never lost hope. It took a long time, many setbacks, but in 1948 we re-established an independent Jewish state.

Quitters are forgotten, but those who hang on will ultimately make the difference.

*The flag of Israel over Masada. This means do not give up*

# Pharaoh's Peace

### December 13, 2015, Israel

It came to pass at the end of two full years that Pharaoh was dreaming, and behold; he was standing by the Nile.

And behold, from the Nile were coming up seven cows, of handsome appearance and robust flesh, and they pastured in the marshland.

And behold, seven other cows were coming up after them from the Nile, of ugly appearance and lean of flesh, and they stood beside the cows on the Nile bank

And the cows of ugly appearance and lean of flesh devoured the seven cows that were of handsome appearance and healthy; then Pharaoh awoke.

And he fell asleep and dreamed again, and behold, seven ears of grain were growing on one stalk, healthy and good

And behold, seven ears of grain, thin and beaten by the east wind, were growing up after them.

And the thin ears of grain swallowed up the seven healthy and full ears of grain; then Pharaoh awoke, and behold, a dream.

Now it came to pass in the morning that his spirit was troubled; so he sent and called all the necromancers of Egypt and all its sages, and Pharaoh related to them his dream, but no one interpreted them for Pharaoh.

Pharaoh woke up in a cold sweat. He had a bad dream, a recurring dream. He tried to sleep but it did not help. He called his trusted advisers and dream interpreters but it left him even more troubled. Seven fat cows, consumed by seven skinny emaciated cows, seven healthy stalks of grain consumed by seven poor ones...what does it mean? One adviser said you will have seven children and all shall die. Pharaoh's spirit was perturbed.

The greatest blessing in life is Peace. That is why the Aharonic priestly blessing ends with the blessing of Peace. He who has peace lacks nothing but the richest man in the world who lacks peace is still a deeply troubled man; Sleepless nights, a tormented soul. No rest for he who has a troubled soul.

So Pharaoh hears of Joseph, a foreigner, a Hebrew, languishing in prison, and rushes him from the dungeon. The Torah stresses how fast this process took. Usually to get someone out of prison is a long process, but Pharaoh was troubled. They cut through all the red tape.

Joseph is presented before the great Pharaoh. Pharaoh says I have heard about you that you can hear a dream and give its meaning.

Joseph answers....*God will restore your peace*. And Pharaoh, like a patient, begins...*In my dream I am standing on the Ye'or...*

Joseph interprets the dream; there will be seven years of plenty, great prosperity in all the land of Egypt, great news. But these will be followed by seven years of famine, and the famine will be so bad that it will be as if there seven years of plenty never were. The good times will be totally forgotten. The prosperity will be totally erased.

The dream has been interpreted, but that is not enough. No, just having this information is not enough to restore the peace of Pharaoh, to allow him a good night's sleep. That is never enough. What is needed is action, action to rectify the situation.

Many people are aware of a situation. They will meet in a coffee house and discuss, complain, till the cows come home, but they will take no action.

Many will cry out "Woe is me, poor me" but what they forget is that after Joseph gave his interpretation of the dream he also advocated action. Without missing a beat he said...and now Pharaoh should appoint a wise man, and many government officials, and they should be stationed throughout the land, and gather up the food during the years of plenty.

Having the interpretation of the dream is not enough. Having knowledge of what will come to pass is not enough. What separates leaders from the rest of us is the taking of action, at once! Many master politicians make their homes in coffee shops. There they preach and sermonize over a good strong cup of coffee. The "Parliament" meets and decides what is best for the country. But of course none of this makes any difference and no one is listening or taking note of the proceedings. The coffee is consumed and everyone goes home.

Action, decisive action, not self-pity. Joseph interpreted the dream, gave practical advice that involved everyone, and took charge of the situation himself. Thus he prevented the people from starving and he saved the kingdom of Pharaoh.

To restore your sense of peace, action will be required.

# It Must Be Right
### DECEMBER 15, 2015, ISRAEL

I am my father's son and I do not forget his lessons. I live his lessons and his teachings.

As a young boy he stressed the lessons of Father Abraham, in Hebrew *Avaraham Avinu*, Abraham the Hebrew, or, Avraham *HaIvri*. Ivri also means Ever...the other side, for Abraham stood on one side of the river with his truth, and the rest of the world stood on the other side of the river with their understanding of the truth. But Abraham would not relent, he did not conform to the majority opinion, he thought for himself.

As my dad taught me, be a majority of one, even if the entire world says you are wrong, it does not matter. God gave you the ability and the responsibility to think for yourself. If not to think then why a brain, a mind. It is to question, to think, to soar.

To be a majority of one, a moral majority, those words have been with me my entire life. My father challenged me, he urged me to think, not to accept blindly.

Today in the world I see that my father's lesson is the exception, not the rule. People believe all sorts of crazy things. You might think, well, they cannot all be wrong, there must be some truth to it, but there is not. Lies take root and are accepted as truth, for many generations.

Much of the world still believes that *"Jews cannot fight"* and that America saved the Jews from the Nazis while the

Jews were only passive victims. In my book "Israel: A Nation of Warriors" I point out the facts, how millions of Jews fought in uniform as part of regular armies on the side of the allies as well as with the partisans. Every ghetto, every concentration camp had its resistance movement. Over half a million Jews fought as part of the United States armed forces, and even more in the Soviet Red Army. Jews fought on all fronts and earned the highest medals for honor and bravery in combat. On *Tour and Train* we visit the monuments that show respect to the Jews who fought and fell as part of the Soviet and Polish armies. Over 200,000 Jews died in the line of service for the USSR, fighting for Mother Russia.

*Monument for the Jewish Polish warriors of World War Two. Mt. Herzl military cemetery, Jerusalem.*

*Tomasz from Poland with Moshe, paying our respect to the warriors, Jews and Poles who fought side by side for freedom. Centuries ago my family escaped the Spanish/Portuguese/Italian persecution and found refuge in Poland.*

And yet lies persist, Jews do not fight, Jews are lazy, Jews do not work hard, Jews live off the hard work of others.

People hear lies and believe, after all, they hear it from their parents, their teachers, their religious leaders, it must be right.

I once heard an interview with an old man. In his youth he was a member of the *HitlerJugend*, the Hitler youth movement. He said very wise words...*we were taught to respect our parents, our elders, we were taught to listen to our religious leaders, they all told us the Jews were bad and must be eliminated from our lives, what should I have believed? Why would I question my parents, my elders?*

This man is correct. What is a child to believe?

And today many millions around the world believe that Jews are descended from apes and pigs and must be killed. While the truth is that many years ago the Jews refused to convert and thus have been targeted for slaughter ever since. Historical truth often conflicts with belief.

Many people are targeted for discrimination, I only use the examples I am most familiar with, I speak as a Jew and extend the lesson to all people. People are taught hatred, they are not born with it, they are indoctrinated with it. They are taught not to question but to kill for "honor", to hate for the cause. And if everyone is going along with it, well, then...it must be right.

Be Abraham, a majority of one. He started as one man, one voice, and he did not give up.

# Better Judgment
### December 15, 2015, Israel, twilight, time for change

Trust your gut feeling. We all have it, we are born with it, call it a gift from God, from nature, but we have it. Animals use it, we suppress it.

We call it our better judgment but usually that phrase is used when people say...I acted against my better judgment.

But why do we do this? Why do we fight our instinct, we know better! We as a people and as individuals act against our better judgment. We destroy ourselves.

Why?

We know we should not eat that extra donut, but we do. We know we should not have that last beer, we already had a few too many, but we do. We know we should not let our bills pile up while we max out on our credit cards, buy new cars and go on vacation, but we do. And then when the proverbial shit hits the fan we say, "I acted against my better judgment'.

We know we must stop certain political movements, we know we must evict certain people from our lives, but we do not. How many people stay in relationships that are totally destructive? How many stay with the abuse? How many remain victims?

We know the answers, we know what we should do, but...we act against our better judgment

We notice suspicious activities, we suspect that someone we know may be up to "no good", but we do not act.

Why? Because it is more comfortable at this particular moment not to act. It takes too much energy to do what we know, with our better judgment, must be done. It is too hard to turn away from that extra piece of cake or that bottle of beer. It is too easy not to take constructive action.

But those who do, those who act in accordance with our better judgment those become the leaders, the doers, the movers and shakers. It is they who build hospitals, it is they who create labor unions, it is they who make change.

It is the likes of Samuel Gompers, Henrietta Szold, Janusz Korczak, Haym Solomon, who make change. Those who rise up, leave the comfort zone, and take action, action that is in our better judgment, action to make this world a better place for all.

But there are many, many, many who wake up each morning with hate, and make no mistake, they are highly motivated. They will not eat that extra donut or drink that beer. They are busy training, to kill you!

Wake up, and act according to your better judgment.

Join a Krav Maga class, you know it is in your better judgment.

# Searching and Finding
### December 16, 2015, Israel

The words of my father are still with me. Certain phrases he liked to use, words of the rabbis that he liked to use in daily conversation. When the words of our ancestors become our own speech, we are blessed and so are they. Imagine, something you said will be part of a conversation taking place between two men two thousand years after your demise, can you imagine that?

In the Babylonian Talmud, we read of Rabbi Isaac, identified as רבי יצחק נפחא "Rabbi Isaac the Smith", as that is what he did for a living. He was born in Israel in the second century but studied in the academies of Babylon; most likely he came into contact with my own ancestors who lived there as well.

He is quoted as saying, If a man tells you 'I have searched hard, I have made an effort and become weary, but I have not found - do not believe him; I have not searched hard but I have found - Do not believe him, I have searched hard and I have found - believe him'"

"אם יאמר לך אדם יגעתי ולא מצאתי – אל תאמין, לא
יגעתי ומצאתי – אל תאמין, יגעתי ומצאתי – תאמין"

My father would quote these words often; it was part of his regular pattern of speech. The idea being that nothing good comes without really searching for it. If someone tells you they came across an amazing discovery but did not toil for it, do not trust them. Good things come with hard work.

If you say I worked hard but did not achieve anything, do not trust these words.

If we were doing homework or reading something, and gave up saying, I do not get it, I did not find it. No, this is unacceptable, go back, look again, for one who says I have searched but have not found is not to be believed. You clearly did not search hard enough, you did not study long enough, you did not delve deep enough. Go back and study!

I have found in our Krav Maga training that many give up easily on a technique. They try it a few times, it did not make perfect sense to them, they were not able to perform it as well as the teacher, so let's drop it, forget it.

They write to me, "This one does not work".

Really? How hard have you tried? How many times did you view the video? How much of an effort did you make? Did you just give it a little causal effort and give up, deciding that the instructor who taught this to you knows nothing? Perhaps you should try harder, dig deeper and try to understand the technique.

Of course we always question and challenge, but in the correct spirit.

Let's go back to the Talmud. Questions and debates are the core of our study. Arguments can get loud and emotional, which is great. But first one has to know what he is talking about. First one must study long and hard, otherwise you just make a fool of yourself. Talmud is the study of law, before one debates in law he must be well versed. It is the same with Krav Maga.

So when someone tells me in a flippant way, *This one does not work,* I smile and laugh and think back to my dear father, I hear his words, the words of Rabbi Isaac the Smith from 1,800 years ago...If one tells you he has searched but not found - Do not believe him.

Rabbi Isaac lived in a generation where the Jews suffered such hardship that he said they fulfilled the Biblical words, *"and you shall eat the grass of the field"* (Genesis, Chapter 3, verse 18) as the people were so hungry they would eat raw grass, and yet he studied and work, and raised the morale of his generation.

Now go and study.

# I Was Sent Before You

December 18, 2015, Israel

Today is my father's birthday; it has been more than eleven years since his passing. My dad, a rabbi, taught me to look at the Torah each time, to read it each time, as if it were the very first time. Let the words speak to you, let them come out. Each time we read the Torah there is a chance that we will learn something new, each time another hidden lesson will come out, one that has perhaps been lying dormant for many years.

Meditate as you read, allow things to happen, and new insights will appear.

Today we read the portion of *WaYigash:* and Judah approached the great Pharaoh. We read about the dramatic and very emotional reunion between Yosef (Joseph) and his long-estranged brothers. The tables have turned, his dreams have come true and now he rules over all the land of Egypt. His brothers bow before him, as he dreamed many years ago as a child in the land of Cana'an. It has all come true.

Now Yosef reassures his brothers: I am not angry at you; this is all part of a great divine plan to save us all from hunger. Do not be upset and do not fear. I am still your brother and I will do you no harm. I will not seek revenge for you having sold me into slavery. For God himself has sent me before you to provide life and substance for all.

> *"Now, therefore be not grieved, nor angry with yourselves, that you sold me here: for*

*God sent me before you to preserve life."*
*(Genesis Chapter 45).*

And now Yosef wastes no time and gets directly to the point. He is here to save them, but first...he must warn them. "For these two years has the famine been in the land, and there are still five more years to come in which there shall neither be ploughing or harvest. And God has sent me before you to preserve you a remnant in the earth, to insure your survival and to save your lives by a great deliverance." (Genesis, Chapter 45)

The message is profound. Let's not argue and bicker over who harmed who, over who is more important, over who came first. I have information that you must understand in order to live, so lets' deal with the issues, lets' deal with survival.

You think things are bad now? Two years of famine! I have news for it and it is not good news, things are only going to get worse, much worse. Things will become very bad before they start turning around and if you do not listen to me, you will not live to see the end of it, you will not survive the next difficult period, for you and all you have, all you have worked for, your families, your household, will all perish and be no longer.

This is a harsh and dire message, but you must listen, or else, you will perish. From the words of the Torah, the Bible, from over 3,500 years ago, a message comes to us which describes our own times, in South Africa, in Israel, in the United States, in Europe. Remember...if you do not take action now, you and all you have shall perish. You will not live to see the end.

Yosef says lets' stop arguing, let's not be angry with each other, for we are brothers. We must deal with the issues ahead and I have a plan that will save you. We must take action now. Listen to what I have to say.

There is always someone sent before you. The Japanese word for teacher is Sensei which is actually two symbols which mean "He who came before you". A teacher is simply one who came before you, one who has been on the path a little bit longer than you. He was sent before you not to dominate you, not to embarrass you, but to guide you, to tell you, in the words of Rabbi Moshe Chaim Luzzatto: "This is the path, follow it", as I have already been through this path.

We must always recognize the messengers in our lives.

Knowing the future is a great advantage. Sadly, we can only take educated guesses. But we see the violence, we see the attacks, we see the writing on the wall, but what do we do? We put a band-aid, a little cream and we say: "All is well".

But there is a Joseph, perhaps he is the local Krav Maga instructor, perhaps he is the voice in the wilderness, and he says...you think this is bad? You are only at the beginning, the worse is yet to come, now listen to me for I have a plan.

But we do not listen to our Joseph; we call him a paranoid prophet of doom. We like the Biblical lessons, but we do not implement them in our lives. We do not apply the lessons.

For the famine has been going on for two years now, but there are still five more years to come where there will be no harvest, no ploughing, now listen to me, or else, you will lose everything.

We have our choice, a messenger was sent before us.

Dedicated to my Dad who always saw the future and always warned about it. His memory is my blessing.

# Awareness Look

### December 20, 2015, Israel

*Random shot, Moshe in the Old City of Jerusalem; awareness.*

We all speak about different levels of alertness. No one can be on guard 24 hours per day, seven days per week. Even soldiers need to take shifts. But when we are in areas known for potential danger, when we are in public places, we need to keep our eyes open.

Unlike other creatures, we are not terribly fast, we cannot turn our necks around, we cannot fly, and we cannot jump or climb trees. Thus, we must use what we have; we must keep our eyes open and be very aware. We must use our intelligence to scan the environment and gather information.

Some people are heavy, some have bad knees and some, walk with canes. They will not be able to run quickly. And yet the mind is sharp and we must learn to be aware, to pick up on subtle clues.

By chance, I noticed a photo of myself, taken during the recent Tour and Train session. At the time, the situation in Israel was a little precarious. We even had our doubts about bringing the group to the Old City of Jerusalem.

I recall that during the entire trip, I was constantly watching...

A. Our group

B. The location and number of Israeli police, military and other security guards

C. Suspicious behavior of certain elements of the population.

Looking at this random photo of myself I notice several points.

1. My eyes are focused like an animal looking for prey.

2. My back is to a safe zone with no space for anyone to get behind me.

3. Behind me is a member of our group, so no suspicious people are near me or behind my back.

4. My hands are in a position where they can rapidly move into an offensive or defensive position.

5. I am balanced, yet, not in an obvious combative position.

This one snapshot captures what I try to teach our students; constant awareness, scanning of the environment, awareness of potential harm and of potential help (paying attention to police, military and security guards, we must know where they are), keeping all members of your group within eyesight and within speaking distance, and watching your back at all times.

# Songs and Guns

### December 20, 2015, Israel

Can guns and songs go together? Can rifles and guitars be slung over the same shoulders? Can you fight for peace?

Yes, the answer is yes.

And this people in Israel raise their voices in song, in prayer, to heaven, to mankind, for peace, for an end to war. A song, a prayer for the soldiers to come home safely, to return from the battle, for this war to be the last war.

I have grown up in this country, every war has its songs, every generation has its songs. Everyone is training for war, but everyone is praying for peace.

From the rabbinical academies reciting the Psalms of King David, to the beatniks on the beaches of Tel Aviv, with the harp and with the guitar, we are all one, and we are all singing the same song.

The smoke is mixed with tears, the gun power is mixed with prayers, it is the sacrifice offered to heaven, no less than that offered by our ancestors on the altar of the Temple.

Brothers go out to war, brothers and sisters, fathers and sons, rockets, bullets, but here we are, we are back home and this people shall never fall back. The spirit of this people shall never be broken.

Images flood the mind, memories fill the heart, different hairstyles, but the spirit is the same, one generation after another, young men walking off to war saying: "Don't' worry, really, there is no reason to worry, I will be home soon."

And we pray for peace. The songs go up to heaven like the sacrifices on the Temple altar, the gun power is the incense of the High Priest, and we pray for no more bloodshed.

Sadness brings songs of hope, and the sound of the shofar, the ram's horn sounds as the old and the new mix. The footsteps continue from one generation to another and we long for the words...All our forces have come home safely, B'Shalom, in peace.

Little boys grow up and become soldiers, little girls grow up and are on the front line supporting them, all too young, all too much. Young men run into battle shouting: "After me", some...never come home and the prayers go up to heaven, another sacrifice. The Levites of old join with the singers of today and the song is one, a song of peace, but a song of war. Put on the uniforms, the warriors of old were anointed with olive oil, the warriors of today wear olive uniforms. And the singers and song writers of the holy city offer their prayers, their songs, a prayer for peace.

A soldier walks off, and we wonder, and we hope and we pray, and we sing. From one generation to another the song remains, a song of hope.

The song is not only words, not only sounds, it is hope, it is spirit, it is the soul.

# Historical Vision

DECEMBER 21, 2015 ISRAEL

Each year at this time, we relive the passing of Patriarch Jacob. Although the events took place about 3,700 years ago, it is still sad. Each year we lose Jacob again. Each year we live through the painful goodbye.

And so Yaakov, Jacob, realizes his time has come and he takes action. He calls his son Yosef, Joseph, a powerful and important man in Egypt, and he gives his final instructions. I will not be buried in the Egypt, I must be brought back to my homeland, I must be buried with my people.

> *"Do not bury me in Egypt. And I will lie with my fathers, and you shall raise me up out of the land of Egypt, and bury me in their burial grounds."(Genesis, Chapter 47, verse 29-30)*

Why the concern? Why does it matter so much? Why is Father Jacob so concerned about what will happen after he leaves this world? He suffered so much in this life, he experienced such deep pain, such painful loss, and now he will finally be at peace, why the concern over his burial place? Why is it so important to him to be buried with his fathers?

To this very day we can visit him, our father Jacob is buried with his fathers Isaac and Abraham in the "disputed" area of Hebron.

History, roots: We know who we are and we know from where we come and where we belong. We fight for the same land as did our forefathers. We live our history, we walk in their footsteps, we plant our vineyards and our olive trees where they planted theirs. We give our children the same names.

Father Jacob knew that life extends beyond his own mortal years; that he must think of the future, of us. No, being buried in the land of Egypt is not an option, he must lie with his fathers, and he must be there for his many children who would come to visit in the years ahead. He must wait for us to come from all the lands of our dispersion. He knew that Israel is our only home and he must be buried there. He knew that we would come to visit him there, if not today, then tomorrow, and if not tomorrow, then the day after, but surely it would come to pass.

We live our history. Abraham, Isaac and Jacob still walk with us, we feel their footsteps, their imprints. We live with our fathers and someday, we will lie with them.

We do not live our life for ourselves alone but for those who came before us and for those who will come long after, we return to dust.

No, I cannot be buried in Egypt Yaakov/Jacob tells his son Yosef/Joseph, you must promise me, you must take an oath that you shall raise me up from the land of exile and return me to our land, our home. Jacob is, also, called Yisrael, Israel, and today we live in the land that is called by his name. And we keep his oath, the oath that he asked Yosef to make. Bring me home!

# Listen Well
### December 22, 2015, Israel

I am thinking of some rabbis that I knew, three in particular, all are no longer among the living. They were special, they were controversial. They were very different, each was special in his own unique way.

One was a fighter, one was a singer, and one was a seer. I had the privilege of meeting all three and seeing their magic.

Magic?

Yes, it was magic, truly it was magic.

I am sitting near a door, Sabbath morning, and he emerges from a door directly across from me, his eye twinkles, his head nods slightly, his silent lips say...Good Shabbos, have a good Sabbath day filled with peace and Joy. It was the Rebbe, back in Brooklyn, A giant of a man. In that one silent moment, he conveyed pure love. What I felt was...You matter, I do not know your name, but you matter, you matter to me so deeply that if need be, I will do everything in my power to help you. And I KNOW this to be true. I have absolute certainty, without the slightest doubt, that if I needed the Rebbe's help, he would have moved heaven and earth to help me. I felt it in his glance.

It is the gift of love, the gift of truly caring.

I am in the back of a room. I am part of the kitchen staff, washing dishes, scrubbing pots and pans, but I know that the Singing Rabbi is in the main hall performing. So I take a little break and sneak a listen. He sees me, there are many people in the audience, but he sees me. He nods towards me and looks directly at me.

Whenever he would meet someone, he would hug them, embrace them, he was pure love. He visited Russia at the time when Jews were not allowed to emigrate, nor were they allowed to practice their religion. It was impossible to purchase Jewish religious objects. So he brought what he could and gave it out for free.

But more people wanted the holy objects. So as he was leaving, he gave his own prayer Shawl, his *tefilin* and even his kipa (yarmulka). He "gave the shirt off his back".

With a man like this you know you are special, you feel special. He makes you feel special.

I was at my first rally. The rabbi came over and spoke to me, he looked at me, it was the Fighting Rabbi and I knew then and there that if need be, he would give his life for me. Over the years, I came to know him very well and he inspired me greatly. When I needed a place to stay, he took me in. He traveled the world warning people about the dangers ahead. He was shot dead in New York City by an Arab. There was no conviction.

What these men had in common was a gift. When you were with them, you felt special. You felt as if you were their only disciple, you felt that you mattered. I am not attaching a photograph to this blog, but this blog was inspired by a photograph. It was a photograph of a young man at my seminar in Germany. He is no longer with us.

The boy felt he needed to leave this life early. Sometimes life...is all too much.

The pain is so great that it has taken me sometime to be able to address this. His father is a man of great spirit and strength. Thank God.

IKI Krav Maga meant so much to him that he was buried in his IKI hoodie and the IKI logo was on his coffin. I can only hope that we added some joy and meaning to his life. At this moment I think of him.

In my father's study there is a plaque, in honor of his father, Grandpa Moe, Moe "Moshe" Katz, of blessed memory. It says God has given, God has taken, let God's name be blessed. The word for given is "Nathan". This was the boys' name. God has given.

I look at the photo of him training. I look at all of us around him and I ask, did we notice him the way those rabbis noticed me? I am not speaking of his family. There is no doubt whatsoever that they loved him unconditionally. My question is for the rest of us. Did we see this young man the way those rabbis saw each and every one of us?

Do we notice others? Do we listen to others?

The Rebbe looked at me with those deep penetrating eyes and I knew I had a guardian angel; life was a little bit better, because I knew that someone cared. I knew that I mattered.

And the singing rabbi who took a moment of his time to look at me, at me! He turned away from his guitar and he looked at me and without saying a word, I know what he was saying..."Moishe, my home is your home, you will never lack for anything, I care about you." I felt it.

We need to care more; we need to see more, we need to feel more. Someone out there needs a word of kindness, a special glance, let us be the one. A smile cost you nothing but a moment of your time.

COMMENTS

Dear Moshe,

First, my condolences. Losing a friend is something I have experienced only once, and it was an awful feeling. I mourn with you, Moshe!

I just read your blog post about your student who committed suicide. During the time I spent with you in Israel you told many good stories and you often spoke of rabbis that had inspired you. I am grateful that you continue to do this through your blog, of which I am a regular reader. As a non-Jewish person I sometimes have to explain to my countrymen why I am inspired by Jewish culture and why I mention rabbis more often than priests. I have no exhaustive and coherent answer but I know that the storytelling is a big part of why. The way that you wrote about this very difficult subject touched me, for I meet many people in my line of work who suffer without anyone having taken notice.

This letter is to express my respect and gratitude for your shining light on a phenomenon that exists in abundance in our modern society. You shared your perspective on your student's tragic passing away and pointed out in a humble tone something that far too few of us even take the time or muster the courage to address or even think about. What is our responsibility as a community, as friends (or strangers for that matter) or as humans to other humans? How can we approach our fellow humans in a manner such that we assuage their discomfort and instil the sense of trust they need to open up to us and allow us to listen or to help? How do we see? Why didn't we see?

Ending this letter I want to say thank you for your choice to stand up for people suffering in silence amidst people who care about them and to whom they could have turned in their difficult situation, were they to know that the people around them weren't ignoring them but were simply for some reason unable to grasp their suffering. And thank you for the humble and warm way in which you did. Unfortunately, as painful as it may be, I think we have to ask ourselves the questions that you ask in your post. That is the only way to improve ourselves and be better prepared the next time a beloved friend or stranger suffers in silence.

I also want to thank you (a very late thank you, I know) for having me as your guest over the Tour and Train. You have inspired me in many ways and taught me so much about self-defense and Jewish culture.

Sincerely yours

**Björn**

# Misunderstandings

December 24, 2015

It is a common refrain...There must be some misunderstanding, there must be some sort of mistake. We all experience this. A relationship is going well, the job is going well, a friendship, a partnership and then, suddenly out of nowhere, it appears to collapse. And we cannot figure out what went wrong.

We rack our brains trying to figure out what we said that changed things. Why would this person turn on me? What could I have said to upset them?

We come up with all sorts of scandalous theories, we stretch our imagination to put together a plausible explanation for what may have happened. We bring other people into our mental game, trying to make sense of it all.

Perhaps it was Joe at the post office who told Alice to throw my package away, because he was upset with me for dating a woman he was after...and *that* is why my package never arrived!

But we avoid the obvious. We avoid just contacting the person directly and asking them: "Did I do something to offend you. I get the feeling that something is wrong, is it all in my imagination or did something happen, because this is killing me and I need my peace of mind."

And usually it all turns out to be one big mistake, a misunderstanding. Someone was busy at work and simply forgot to take care of something that they had promised you. There is always a logical explanation. Perhaps it was a language issue, someone not speaking English as a first language, or a cultural issue.

But what do we normally do? We stew in it. We let it kill us. We get all upset. That ….good for nothing, low down scum, how could he?

We build a war in our heads when all we needed to do was pick up the phone. And if there really is an issue, now we can deal with it. But usually it is nothing.

I have been on both sides of this. Innocent off hand remarks were misunderstood and blown out of proportion. Only months later a friend who said to me: "Moshe, I have a bone to pick with you." and I would have absolutely no clue what it was about.

And I have also been the one wondering why someone was "upset" with me. But then I remembered this lesson and I picked up the phone, had a little chat and realized how foolish I was. The person would say: "Oh yes, I forgot to send you that, end of the year, so busy with work, it just slipped my mind". And all is well.

And then I reprimand myself; why did I allow myself to be upset for a few days? Why did I not contact this person earlier? I wasted good energy being upset and troubled over nothing.

Sometimes we just fear people's reactions, we do not want to come across as "too pushy". I have a dear friend who never wants to talk to anyone on the plane. Fair enough. He hates it when someone strikes up a conversation. So he puts up his defense; earphones, blanket over his head, he makes it clear.

But at other times, why not strike up a conversation. Why not meet somebody fascinating whom you may never have a chance to meet again? I have gained incredible wisdom from some strangers with whom I shared a flight.

I had the privilege of spending time with the amazing late great Rabbi Weinberg of blessed memory. He said: "You want to talk to the person sitting next to you? Turn to them and say Hello! What is the worst that can happen? They will say 'I do not want to talk' but if you do have a conversation, it can be a pleasant way to pass the time and learn something interesting."

I have learned not to be afraid to speak up, to a friend, or a stranger. Muster up the courage, open your mouth and just say it; you can avoid and resolve a great deal of painful misunderstandings.

So as we approach the year 2016, let us resolve to clear up misunderstandings, do a Spring Cleaning of our anger and frustrations, pick up the phone and clear the waves of communication.

# Dare to Be Different

December 29, 2015, Israel

Life pushes us towards conformity. Most immigrant children soon look and sound just like their local pears. People want to fit in. Those who are different are marked. In his classic work, "The Painted Bird", Jerzy Kosinski describes how children caught a bird, painted it and then released it to the wild. The bird quickly rejoined its flock; birds of a feather flock together. But the other birds did not accept the returned member. He now was different. They poked him to death. The young boy learned a valuable lesson.

Kosiński was a Polish Jew, born Józef Lewinkopf in Łódź, Poland. His father gave him a false name to help him survive the Holocaust. With the assistance of righteous Polish villagers and a priest, he survived the war and immigrated to America. He had learned what it is like to be different. To survive, one had to fit in.

People who are different stand out and sometimes, pay for it dearly. The harsh payment can be in terms of losing one's job, or losing one's friends, or in extreme cases, losing one's life. Standing up and saying: "The king has no clothes" while everyone else is shouting: "The king has new clothes", can lead to severe social ostracism or worse.

But change occurs when someone dares to be different. And sometimes when one person stands up for the truth, others follow. There are others who are waiting for a leader, waiting for someone to take the initiative, the first steps. And then others stand up and say: "I was thinking that too!! Let's do something about it."

We need someone who dares to be different. We need people to stand up and speak, no matter the potential consequences. Truth needs only an army of one.

Many people offer "what the people want to hear"; it is safe, they are breaking no new ground. They want to offer a proven product, a proven winner. If a new employee suggests something radically different, the CEO might say, Stop, we do not want to rock the boat, *"if it ain't broke, don't fix it"*.

But another company will launch a new product, something different, something innovative, and .... the world changes.

Believe it or not, there were those who thought the automobile (cars) would never replace the horse and buggy. There were those who thought a tape recording device was fun, but had no practical use. There were those who thought the world market for computers would peak at five!

There were those who thought the idea of a telephone in one's home would never catch on, and many record companies turned down the Beatles, many publishing companies turned down the Harry Potter novels.

But someone dared to be different. Someone said the Beatles have a new sound which I believe will catch on, and the music world was changed forever.

If no one dared to be different, we would still be living as we did in Dark Ages. We would be using the same "technologies", have the same life expectancy and hold the same outrageous beliefs.

We are approaching "New Years' Day" celebrated the world over and even in Israel under the name Sylvester Day. I dared to expose the truth. As much as I know that it has become a fun, mostly secular and universal holiday, I felt the need to say the truth. I believed that I would encounter some resistance, some anger, but the truth needs only an army of one.

So I wrote a little bit about the history of this day as it pertains to the Jewish people. For us it is a sad time filled with terrible memories of hatred, persecution and murder. The day is named for Sylvester, an anti-Semite who convinced the Roman emperor to decree that no Jew should live in Jerusalem. Sylvester arranged for the passage of a host of viciously anti-Semitic legislation and this day, New Year's Day, became a day of hatred and violence towards the Jews for many centuries to come.

I published this fully expecting a backlash. After all, no one enjoys hearing the ugly side of their history and Jews certainly do not want to hear that they should not celebrate New Years'. Amazingly enough it was received very positively. Many shared this posting and many thanked me for it.

Dare to be different, dare to join the army of truth, even if you are an army of one, and the world will be a better place for it.

### *Krav Maga Applications*

What we offer is different, we are not just another organization, we are not just improving techniques. We take a new approach, somewhat revolutionary. Concepts over techniques, mind over body, reality over sport. For all people, all ages, all times; IKI, Israeli Krav International, we dare to be different.

# Memories and Lessons

### December 31, 2015, Israel

Lessons are everywhere. Life is an ongoing process of learning. If you are still alive it is a sign you are still meant to be learning. We are in the school of life, forever.

Lessons are strange. I am still learning from my high school and college experience. Yes, amazing, I am still learning, but not what I thought I would be learning. When I was in university I focused on the Cold War, the stock market, theories of markets, Marx and Engels, Hobbes and Rousseau, but other lessons would come, years later.

Years later, decades later, lessons would sink in: A man who has wisdom but not the ability to explain it, cannot be a teacher. A teacher is not necessarily one who "can do" but one who can give. A teacher focuses on others, a champion focuses on himself.

Grades mean nothing. Years later we do not remember our grades, all we remember are life lessons. Knowledge fades, teachers who only gave you knowledge are soon forgotten, but a teacher who inspired you to study, to search, is with you for life. I can still see Rabbi Cohen, his eyes full of life, pounding on the table, "But why?" Rabbi Heisler's eyes seemed to be in the world of the scholars, and Rabbi Wehls' eyes imploring you to find the truth, to set priorities, uncompromising, a man on a mission.

My teachers gave me a love for truth, for the analytical study that comes from Talmud, for the beauty of knowing your history and the thirst for knowledge.

Humility: I studied with some world renowned geniuses, only I did not know it at the time. They were devoid of ego. At times they had to put me in my place, years later I thank them. They challenged me and made me fight for my point of view. These are lessons that we appreciate years later.

I can picture some of my teachers, men and women of stature, full of passion, sharp and insightful.

But there is more, there are living memories. There is that look in the eye of a teacher that draws you into his personal memories, his passions, and takes you to places you have never been, to experience what he experienced, to see a life from long ago, to see a world you never lived in, to feel what you have never felt before.

Through the eyes of a teacher, you can travel to the distant past or to an unimagined future.

A rabbi stands in front of you, but he has one foot firmly planted in the past and one stretching into the future as he speaks with the fervor of a prophet. His memories go back to fires of Auschwitz, to the synagogues of Poland, to the expulsion from Spain, to the destruction of the Temple, to the forefathers of our people. We remember and we live it.

My memories extend far beyond my own limited lifetime. My life lessons are not only from my own limited experiences. With me is the immigrant experience of my grandparents, the Brooklyn experience of my father, dreams and hopes, what is was like growing up before we had the State of Israel, the Third Jewish commonwealth.

I see the pain of the Shtetel Jew; the Jew living in poverty in small villages throughout Europe. But I see the beauty and the joy as well, the rich heritage. I see the Jew who worked all day everyday, but when the holy Sabbath came, no matter how poor he was, he became a king, he raised his cup of wine and his voice soared to heaven. He debated the meaning of life with others, as if the world depended on it. I see the Jew who clutched his holy books for dear life, cherishing them as the precious jewels that they are, for he who has wisdom lacks nothing.

I see the glory of mankind and the humility. The memories become the lessons; The quest, to search for more, to hunger for answers. The look in a teacher's eye, the look that stays with you forever, that never dies even when our teachers pass from this earth. A sparkle, a hint of pain, but a hint of love, a soul.

The softness in the eyes of a parent; our first and most important teachers, they are with us forever in eternity.

Printed in Great Britain
by Amazon